With many thanks to
John Fitzgerald, Rebecca McCormick,
and Sheliah Shepard

Dedicated with love to:

John Joel Fitzgerald, my husband,
and Amanda Therese Fitzgerald, our daughter
(December 5, 1981–March 31, 2002)

MATH DICTIONARY

FOR KIDS

THE #1 GUIDE FOR HELPING KIDS WITH MATH

THERESA R. FITZGERALD

Prufrock Press

Waco, Texas

Library of Congress Cataloging-in-Publication Data

Names: Fitzgerald, Theresa R. (Theresa Rose), 1962- | Compton, Lacy, editor.
Title: Math dictionary for kids : the #1 guide for helping kids with math.
Description: 5th edition. | Waco, Texas : Prufrock Press, Inc., [2016] |
  Subtitle varies slightly from previous edition. | Edited by Lacy Compton.
  | Includes index.
Identifiers: LCCN 2016016522 | ISBN 9781618216175 (pbk.)
Subjects: LCSH: Mathematics--Dictionaries, Juvenile.
Classification: LCC QA5 .F58 2016 | DDC 510.3--dc23
LC record available at https://lccn.loc.gov/2016016522

Edited by Lacy Compton

Layout design by Raquel Trevino

ISBN-13: 978-1-61821-617-5

Printed in the United States of America.

At the time of this book's publication, all facts and figures cited are the most current available. All telephone numbers, addresses, and website URLs are accurate and active. All publications, organizations, websites, and other resources exist as described in the book, and all have been verified. The author and Prufrock Press Inc. make no warranty or guarantee concerning the information and materials given out by organizations or content found at websites, and we are not responsible for any changes that occur after this book's publication. If you find an error, please contact Prufrock Press Inc.

Prufrock Press Inc.
P.O. Box 8813
Waco, TX 76714-8813
Phone: (800) 998-2208
Fax: (800) 240-0333
http://www.prufrock.com

TABLE OF CONTENTS

INTRODUCTION

Every discipline has its own unique vocabulary, a group of words and definitions that people use to study or communicate information within that field. The key to understanding any subject is knowing its terminology. Likewise, mathematics has a vocabulary, consisting of words and symbols, that allows people to have a common base of understanding. And, like other disciplines, knowing the vocabulary of mathematics gives one the power to unlock problems.

There are many keys to being a proficient math problem solver, and two of the most important elements to successful problem solving are knowing:

- what the problem is asking (understanding the vocabulary and being able to determine which strategy to employ), and
- how to perform the operation(s) (being able to quickly and automatically perform the necessary operations).

Besides providing information that will help math students in these two important areas of problem solving, this math dictionary also offers a wealth of other information, compiled in an easy-to-use format.

The *Math Dictionary for Kids* is much more than a compilation of words and definitions. This book has been organized to reflect the different areas of mathematics taught in elementary and junior high schools. Each category includes the terms commonly used in this field of study, concise definitions, and many examples and illustrations. In addition, the book provides quick reference guides for basic operations and tables of commonly used facts and equivalents.

This is a book that should be used throughout the year. It can be used on a daily basis in the whole-class setting to review the vocabulary and operations associated with the math unit being studied. This daily review provides continuous reinforcement that leads to proficiency. The book can also be used on an individual basis. A student can take it out of his or her desk as a reference to check what a term means or how an operation is performed. This cuts down on the chances of making mistakes, aids comprehension, and builds self-reliance.

Once you use a reference like this book, you'll agree that it truly is absolutely essential. It will be the reference material you will use again and again to supplement and reinforce each topic in your mathematics curriculum.

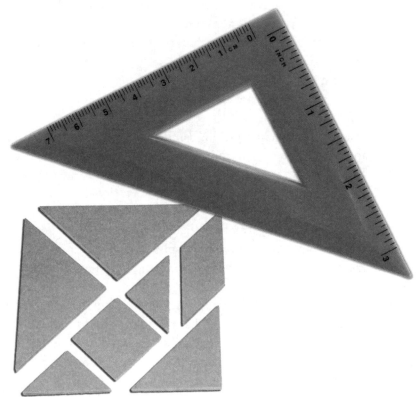

WHOLE NUMBERS AND OPERATIONS

Addends

Numbers in addition problems that are added together to form a sum.

Example:
3 + 7 = 10
3 and 7 are addends.

Addition

The process of uniting two or more numbers into a sum; counting the total.
Key word: altogether

Examples:

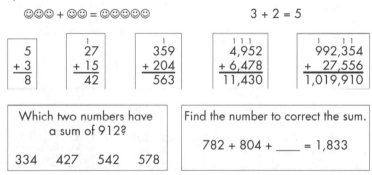

☺☺☺ + ☺☺ = ☺☺☺☺☺   3 + 2 = 5

5 + 3 8	$\overset{1}{27}$ + 15 42	$\overset{1}{359}$ + 204 563	$\overset{1\,1\,1}{4,952}$ + 6,478 11,430	$\overset{1\quad1\,1}{992,354}$ + 27,556 1,019,910

Which two numbers have a sum of 912?	Find the number to correct the sum.
334 427 542 578	782 + 804 + ____ = 1,833

Arabic Numbers

A Base-10 place-value number system that uses the symbols 0, 1, 2, 3, 4, 5, 6, 7, 8, and 9. Also called Hindu-Arabic numbers.

Arithmetic Progression

A series of numbers in which each number differs from the preceding number by a fixed amount. A series of numbers that follows a pattern.

Example:
1, 5, 9, 13, 17, 21, 25, 29, . . .
Each number differs by 4.

Array

An organized arrangement of objects using rows and columns. These can be very helpful in building multiplication problems and division problems.

Example 1:
6 rows of 7 columns = 42 squares altogether
6 × 7 = 42

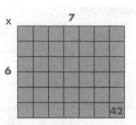

Example 2:
1. Build the problem 20 ÷ 4 in an array using as many of the 20 tiles as you can.
2. Count the number of rows that have been built, and count the remainder.
3. 20 ÷ 4 = 5. There is no remainder in this problem.

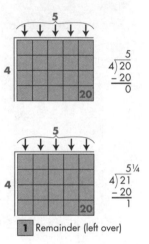

Example 3:
1. Count out 21 tiles.
2. Build the problem 21 ÷ 4 in an array using as many of the 20 tiles as you can.
3. In this case, 20 tiles can be used to build the array with 1 tile left over.
4. Count the number of rows that have been built, and count the remainder.
5. 20 ÷ 4 = 5. There is 1 remainder. Write the remainder as a fraction. 21 ÷ 4 = 5¼

1 Remainder (left over)

Ascend

To increase in number, value, or amount.

Ascending Order

Increasing from least to greatest, but not necessarily according to a fixed pattern. To count upward from smallest to largest; counting up.

Examples:
35, 37, 39, 41, 43, 45, 47, 49, . . .
An example of an ascending arithmetic progression.

1, 5, 13, 40, 53
A series of numbers in ascending order.

Binary Numbers

A numerical system that is based on the number 2. Each place has a value equal to a power of 2, as indicated or shown by the symbols 0 or 1.

Base 10	1	2	3	4	5	6	7	8	9
Base 2	1	10	11	100	101	110	111	1000	1001

Cardinal Numbers

Numbers used for counting or answering the question "how many?"; they show quantity.
Key words: counting numbers

Example:
Numbers such as 1, 2, 3, 47, and 104 are cardinal numbers.

Common Factor/Common Divisor

A factor that two or more numbers have in common. A number that divides two or more numbers evenly (without a remainder).

Example 1:
When using tiles to look at two numbers, the common factors are the factors that both numbers share.

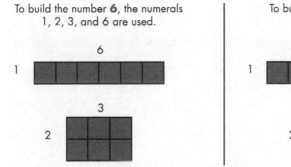

To build the number **6**, the numerals 1, 2, 3, and 6 are used.

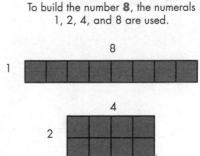

To build the number **8**, the numerals 1, 2, 4, and 8 are used.

The factors that 6 and 8 have in common, or share, are 1 and 2.

Example 2:

①②3, and 6 are the factors of 6.
①②4, and 8 are the factors of 8.

The factors that 6 and 8 have in common, or share, are 1 and 2.

Common Multiple

Any number that is a multiple of two or more numbers; a multiple that two or more numbers have in common, or share.

Key words: common, shared

Example:

Multiples of 2	2	4	6	8	10	**12**	14	16	18	. . .
Multiples of 3	3	6	9	**12**	15	18	21	24	27	. . .
Multiples of 4	4	8	**12**	16	20	24	28	32	36	. . .
Multiples of 5	5	10	15	20	25	30	35	40	45	. . .
Multiples of 6	6	**12**	18	24	30	36	42	48	54	. . .

12 is a common multiple of 2, 3, 4, and 6.

Composing Numbers

The process of creating a larger number through addition.

Example:
1,000 + 300 + 10 + 7 is composed as 1,317.

Composite Number

A number that has factors other than 1 and itself. A number that can be built in more than one way using tiles. Composite numbers can be written as the product of prime numbers.

Example:

The number **6** is composite because there is more than one way to build it.

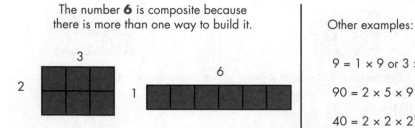

Other examples:

9 = 1 × 9 or 3 × 3

90 = 2 × 5 × 9

40 = 2 × 2 × 2 × 5

Counting Numbers

The positive whole numbers. Also called natural numbers.

Example:
1, 2, 3, 4, 5, . . .

Decline

To decrease in number, value, or amount.

Decomposing Numbers

The process of separating a number into its component parts.

Example:
3,487 can be decomposed as 3,000 + 400 + 80 + 7.

Decrease

To make less (smaller).

Descending Order

Decreasing from greatest to least, but not necessarily in a fixed pattern. To count downward from largest to smallest.

Example:
101, 90, 87, 72, 56
A series of numbers in descending order.

Difference

The answer to a subtraction problem.

Example:
7 – 5 = 2
2 is the difference between the numbers.

Dividend

The number in division that is to be divided, or broken, into equal parts.

Example:

$$\begin{array}{r} 5 \\ 6\overline{)30} \end{array} \text{ or } 30 \div 5 = 6$$

30 is the dividend.

Divisibility Rules

2 A number is divisible by 2 if it is even or if the last digit is divisible by 2.

3 A number is divisible by 3 if the sum of its digits is divisible by 3.

4 A number is divisible by 4 if the number formed by the last two digits is divisible by 4 or if the last two digits are two zeros.

5 A number is divisible by 5 if its last digit is 5 or zero.

6 A number is divisible by 6 if the number is even and is divisible by 3.

Divisibility Rules, continued

9 A number is divisible by 9 if the sum of its digits is divisible by 9.

10 A number is divisible by 10 if its last digit is a zero.

Divisible

Capable of being divided evenly without leaving a remainder.

Example:
20 ÷ 4 = 5
20 is divisible by 4.

Division

The process of division, meaning:

1. Breaking a number into smaller groups of equal quantities.
2. Repeated subtraction; subtracting the same number again and again.
3. Breaking a number into an equal amount of same-sized pieces.

Key words: evenly divided, evenly split, evenly shared between or among, fair shares, even groups of, how many would each get . . ., divisor, dividend, quotient, remainder, left over, fraction

Example:

$$4\overline{)12}^{\,3}$$

4 is the divisor, 12 is the dividend, and 3 is the quotient.

Division Strategies

✪ Larger Numbers: Multiples Table

1. Make a multiples table (see p. 9) for the number you are dividing by, the divisor.
2. Subtract the largest multiple of the divisor that does not exceed the dividend.
3. When you can't subtract any more multiples of 100s, begin subtracting multiples of 10s, and then multiples of 1 through 9.
4. When you can't subtract any more multiples, add the number of multiples that have been subtracted. This final number is the quotient.

Division Strategies, continued
✪ Larger Numbers: Multiples Table, continued

Multiples Table for 34

1	34	11	374
2	68	20	680
3	102	30	1,020
4	136	40	1,360
5	170	50	1,700
6	204	60	2,040
7	238	70	2,380
8	272	80	2,720
9	306	90	3,060
10	340	100	3,400

$$
\begin{array}{r}
100+80+3 \\
34\overline{)6243} \\
-3400 \\
\hline
2843 \\
-2720 \\
\hline
123 \\
-102 \\
\hline
21
\end{array}
$$

Answer: 183 r 21

✪ Repeated Subtraction

23 was subtracted a total of four
imes with 6 remaining, so the
answer is **4 r 6** or **4 %23**.

$$
\begin{array}{r}
4\frac{6}{23} \text{ or } 4 \text{ r } 6 \\
23\overline{)98} \\
-23 \\
\hline
75 \\
-23 \\
\hline
52 \\
-23 \\
\hline
29 \\
-23 \\
\hline
6
\end{array}
$$

9

WHOLE NUMBERS AND OPERATIONS

Division Strategies, continued

✪ Use Manipulatives

Use beans, counters, or other objects, or draw a picture. Count out the number of beans that need to be divided. Divide them equally into the number of groups that are you are dividing by.

$43 \div 6 = 7 \text{ r } 1$

Use tiles or paper squares. Count out the number of tiles that need to be divided. Put them into the number of rows you are dividing by. Count the number of columns you make, and then count the remainder.

$13 \div 5 = 2 \text{ r } 3$

5 Rows

Divisor

The number in a division problem by which the dividend is divided. The number used to divide by.

Example:

$$4\overline{)28}^{\,7}$$

or $28 \div 4 = 7$ **4** is the divisor.

Double

To count something twice.
Twice as much.

Example:
Double 3 means the same thing as
3 + 3 = 6 or 3 x 2 = 6.

Equal

Having the same value in quantity, size, or amount.

Example:

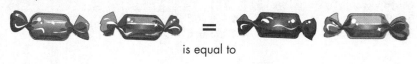

is equal to

Equality

The property of being equal. The following are true of equal numbers:

*   a = a
*   If a = b, then b = a
*   If a = b and b = c, then a = c

Even Number

A whole number that has 0, 2, 4, 6, or 8 in the ones place. It can be divided evenly into two equal groups with no remainder. Even numbers are divisible by 2.

Example:
14 is an even number; when put into two equal groups, there is no remainder.

Expanded Form

Numbers broken up into their individual place values.

Example:
$$3,422 = 3,000 + 400 + 20 + 2$$
$$= (3 \times 1,000) + (4 \times 100) + (2 \times 10) + 2$$
$$= (3 \times 10^9) + (4 \times 10^2) + (2 \times 10^1) + (2 \times 10^0)$$

Fact Family

A group of addition and subtraction or multiplication and division facts made from the same three numbers.

Examples:
Addition/Subtraction (3, 7, 10)

7 + 3 = 10	10 – 3 = 7
3 + 7 = 10	10 – 7 = 3

Multiplication/Division (3, 8, 24)

3 x 8 = 24	24 ÷ 8 = 3
8 x 3 = 24	24 ÷ 3 = 8

Factor

One of two or more numbers that are multiplied together to get a product (the answer).

Example:
6 x 7 = 42
6 and **7** are factors of 42.

Factorial

The product of consecutive numbers, always starting with the number 1. It is symbolized by using an exclamation point (!).

Examples:
3! = 1 x 2 x 3 = 6
6! = 1 x 2 x 3 x 4 x 5 x 6 = 720

Fewer

A smaller number of objects or things.

Example:

is fewer than

Greater

A larger numbers of objects or things.

Example:

is greater than

Greater Than/Less Than

A way of comparing two groups of objects using the symbols > and <. The symbols for greater than and less than can be remembered in these ways:

Two are greater than one. The side with two ends points toward the larger number.

Mouths with sharp teeth like to take bigger bites!

Example: 8 < 11

Greatest Common Factor (GCF)

The largest number that is a common factor, or divisor, of two numbers.

Example:
Factors of 30: **1**, **2**, **3**, 5, **6**, 10, 15, 30
Factors of 24: **1**, **2**, **3**, 4, **6**, 8, 12, 24
1, **2**, **3**, and **6** are the common factors of 24 and 30. The greatest common factor is 6.

Hindu-Arabic Numbers

A Base-10 place-value number system that uses the symbols 0, 1, 2, 3, 4, 5, 6, 7, 8, and 9. Also called Arabic numbers.

Increase

To make more (larger).

Infinite

Having so many that the quantity is unable to be measured or counted. The symbol for infinity is ∞. Infinite sets are also noted with the symbol . . . , which means that the numbers go on and on forever.

Example:
2, 4, 6, 8, 10, 12, . . .

Integer

Another way to name whole numbers and zero. Integers can be either positive or negative, but they do not include fractions, mixed numbers, or decimals.

Examples:
5, 17, and 487
Examples of positive integers.

–334, –15, –3, and –1
Examples of negative integers.

½, **3¼**, and **.09** are not examples of integers because they are not whole numbers.

Inverse Operation

The opposite operation. Subtraction is the inverse of addition, and division is the inverse of multiplication.

Irrational Numbers

Numbers that can be written as decimals but not as fractions. These decimals do not repeat or terminate.

Examples:
The square root of $2 = \sqrt{2} = 1.41421 \ldots$
The square root of $3 = \sqrt{3} = 1.73205 \ldots$
pi $(\pi) = 3.14159 \ldots$

Laws of Arithmetic

There are several laws that govern basic arithmetic operations.

✪ Associative Law (Grouping Property)

Changing the way the addends or factors are grouped does not change the sum or the product.

Examples:
Addition
$(a + b) + c = a + (b + c)$
$(4 + 9) + 1 = 4 + (9 + 1)$

Multiplication
$(a \times b) \times c = a \times (b \times c)$
$(2 \times 5) \times 10 = 2 \times (5 \times 10)$

✪ Commutative Law (Order Property)

Changing the order of the addends does not change the sum or product.

Examples:
Addition
$a + b = b + a$
$7 + 12 = 12 + 7$

Multiplication
$a \times b = b \times a$
$3 \times 8 = 8 \times 3$

Laws of Arithmetic, continued

✪ Distributive Law

A number that is multiplied by the sum of two or more numbers is the same as the sum of that number multiplied by each of the numbers separately.

Example:
$$a \times (b + c) = (a \times b) + (a \times c)$$
$$2 \times (3 + 4) = (2 \times 3) + (2 \times 4)$$

✪ Zero Property of Addition

Any number plus zero equals that number.

Example:
$$467 + 0 = 467$$
$$-8 + 0 = -8$$

✪ Zero Property of Multiplication

Any number multiplied by zero equals zero.

Examples:
$$7 \times 0 = 0$$
$$0 \times 33 = 0$$
$$-5 \times 0 = 0$$

Less Than/Greater Than

See *Greater Than/Less Than*.

Lowest Common Multiple (LCM)

The lowest multiple that two or more numbers have in common.

Example:
Multiples of 2:   2   4   **6**   8   10   **12**   14   16   **18**   20   22   **24** . . .
Multiples of 3:   3   **6**   9   **12**   15   **18**   21   **24**   27   30   33   36 . . .

6, **12**, **18**, and **24** are all multiples of 2 and 3, but 6 is the lowest common multiple because it is the first number that is in both sets.

Minuend

A number from which another number is subtracted.

Example:
$$23 - 5 = 18$$
23 is the minuend.

Multiple

A number that is the product of a specific number and another whole number. The numbers said when counting by the same number repeatedly.

Examples:
2 x 6 = 12
12 is a multiple of 2 and 6.

Count by 3:
3, 6, 9, 12, 15, 18, 21, . . .
The numbers are multiples of 3.

MULTIPLES OF	1	2	3	4	5	6	7	8	9
1	1	2	3	4	5	6	7	8	9
2	2	4	6	8	10	12	14	16	18
3	3	6	9	12	15	18	21	24	27
4	4	8	12	16	20	24	28	32	36
5	5	10	15	20	25	30	35	40	45
6	6	12	18	24	30	36	42	48	54
7	7	14	21	28	35	42	49	56	63
8	8	16	24	32	40	48	56	64	72
9	9	18	27	36	45	54	63	72	81

Multiplication

Repeated addition. Adding the same number a given number of times. Key words: total, in all, altogether, _____ groups of _____, area, product, factor, multiples, square, prime, composite, square root

Example:
4 x 3 = 12 is the same as
3 + 3 + 3 + 3 = 12.
They are both four groups of 3.

Multiplication Patterns

Multiplying and Dividing With Ending Zero: Having one or more zeros at the end of a problem can help when you see the pattern.

✪ **Multiplying with zero in one factor:**

6 x 4 = 24   6 x 4,000 = 24,000
6 x 40 = 240   6 x 40,000 = 240,000
6 x 400 = 2,400   6 x 400,000 = 2,400,000

Multiplication Patterns, continued

✪ Multiplying with zero in one factor, continued

How to do it: If only one factor ends in zeros, count them all and record them in the answer space. Multiply the remaining numbers and write them in the answer to finish the problem.

9 x 30,000 = 0000 (There are 4 zeros at the end, so write them in the answer.)
9 x 30,000 = 27, so the final answer is **270,000**

✪ Multiplying with zero in both factors:

60 x 40 = 2,400	60 x 4,000 = 240,000
600 x 40 = 24,000	600 x 40,000 = 24,000,000
600 x 400 = 240,000	60 x 400,000 = 24,000,000

How to do it: If both factors end in zeros, count them all and record them in the answer space. Multiply the remaining numbers and write them in the answer to finish the problem.

8,000 x 40,000 = 0,000,000 (There are 7 zeros at the end, so write them in the answer.)
8,000 x 40,000 = 32, so the final answer is **320,000,000**

✪ Dividing with zero in the dividend:

28 ÷ 4 = 7	28,000 ÷ 4 = 7,000
280 ÷ 4 = 70	280,000 ÷ 4 = 70,000
2,800 ÷ 4 = 700	2,800,000 ÷ 4 = 700,000

How to do it: If dividend has zeros at the end, count them all and record them in the answer space. Cross them off in the dividend to keep from getting confused. Divide the remaining numbers as normal and write them in the answer to finish the problem.

27,~~000~~ ÷ 9 = 000 (There are 3 zeros at the end, so write them in the answer.)
27 ÷ 9 = 3, so the final answer is **3,000**
Proof: 3,000 x 9 = 27,000

✪ Dividing with zero in the dividend and the divisor:

280 ÷ 40 = 7	28,000 ÷ 400 = 7,000
2800 ÷ 40 = 70	280,000 ÷ 40,000 = 70,000

How to do it: If dividend and the divisor have zeros at the end, count only the number of zeros they have in common. Cross them off in the dividend and divisor to keep from getting confused. Divide the remaining numbers as normal and write them in the answer to finish the problem.

18~~0~~ ÷ 2~~0~~ = (They have 1 zero at the end in common, so cross them off.)
18~~0~~ ÷ 2~~0~~ = 9, so the final answer is **9**
Proof: 9 x 20 = 180

WHOLE NUMBERS AND OPERATIONS

Multiplication Patterns, continued

✪ Dividing with zero in the dividend and the divisor, continued

36,000 ÷ 90 =   (They have 1 zero in common, so cross them off.)
36,000 ÷ 90 = 400, so the final answer is **400**
Proof: 400 x 90 = 36,000

28,000 ÷ 400 =   (They have 2 zeros in common; cross them off.)
28,000 ÷ 400 = 70, so the final answer is **70**
Proof: 70 x 400 = 28,000

Multiplication Strategies

✪ Break Apart

Example:
4 x 6 =   2 x 6 = 12
           2 x 6 = 12
           12 + 12 = 24

✪ Break Apart (Larger Numbers)

Example:

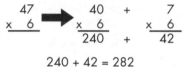

240 + 42 = 282

✪ "Count By" Using Multiples

Example:
6 + 6 + 6 + 6 = 24
      or
6   12   18   24

✪ Crossed Lines (Count Intersections)

Example:

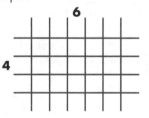

✪ Draw a Picture

Example:

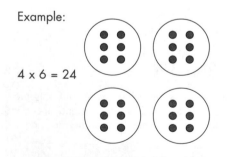

4 x 6 = 24

✪ Window Pane Math

Example:
63 x 24 = 1,512

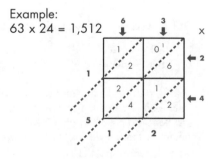

Numbers, Sets of

Natural or counting numbers	{1, 2, 3, 4, 5, 6, . . .}
Whole numbers	{0, 1, 2, 3, 4, 5, 6, . . .}
Integers	{. . . ,–4, –3, –2, –1, 0, 1, 2, 3, 4, . . .}
Negative integers	{. . . , –7, –6, –5, –4, –3, –2, –1}
Positive integers	{1, 2, 3, 4, 5, 6, 7, 8, . . .}
Rational numbers	the set of integers, as well as numbers that can be written as proper and improper fractions
Irrational numbers	the set of numbers that can be written as decimals but not as fractions

Numeral

A word or symbol used to represent a number.

Example:
The numeral 7 represents seven things.

Odd Number

A whole number that has a 1, 3, 5, 7, or 9 in the ones place. When divided into two groups, there will be a remainder.

Example:
15 is an odd number; when put into two equal groups, there is a remainder.

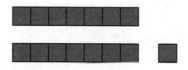

Order of Operations

A set of rules agreed upon by mathematicians that outline the steps to take when solving multioperational problems. These rules help reduce confusion when solving problems and ensure that the same answer can be reached every time.

Order of Operations, continued

Sometimes it helps to remember PEMDAS. "**P**lease **E**xcuse **M**y **D**ear **A**unt **S**ally" stands for:

1. Complete the work in **parentheses** (or brackets) first.
2. Simplify **exponents**.
3. **Multiply** or **divide** from left to right.
4. **Add** or **subtract** from left to right.

Example:
$6^2 + 15 \times (1 + 3) \div 5 =$
$6^2 + 15 \times 4 \div 5 =$
$36 + 15 \times 4 \div 5 =$
$36 + 60 \div 5 =$
$36 + 12 = 48$

Sometimes problems may not have all of the components listed above (parentheses, exponents, multiplication/division, and addition/subtraction). If so, continue down the list of steps until you reach a step that fits the problem.

Example:
$9 - 3 + 2 \times 6 =$ There are no parentheses or exponents,
$9 - 3 + 12 =$ so begin with Step 3 of PEMDAS.
$6 + 12 = 18$

Ordinal Numbers

Numbers that express degree, quality, or position. Numerals that show order.

Example:
First, second, third   Examples of ordinal numbers.
1, 2, 3   Examples of cardinal numbers.

Pair

A set or sets of two. Two of a kind.

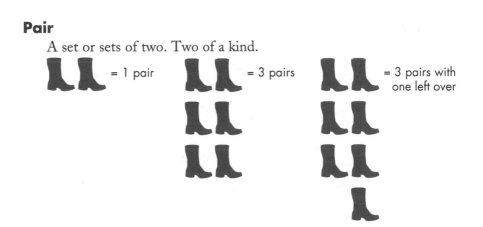

Periods

A way to name the groups of three numbers that make up place value.

Trillions Period	Billions Period	Millions Period	Thousands Period	Units (Ones) Period
— — —	, — — —	, — — —	, — — —	, — — —

Place Value

The value given to the space a digit holds because of its place in a numeral. These values are named according to the spot each takes up.

Example:

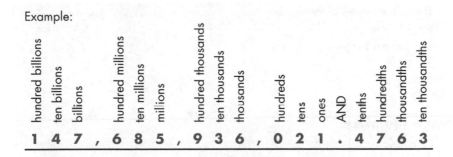

Prime Factors

Prime numbers that, when multiplied, will result in a given number. Use division to find the prime factors of a number.

Example:
The prime factors of the number 16 are circled.

16 can be divided by 2 evenly. Two is a prime number, but 8 can be divided again.

4 can be divided further.

The **prime factors** of 16 are **2, 2, 2,** and **2**.

16 = 2 x 2 x 2 x 2

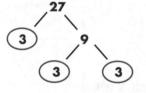

Example:
The prime factors of the number 27 are circled.

The **prime factors** of 27 are **3, 3,** and **3**.

27 = 3 x 3 x 3

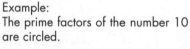

Example:
The prime factors of the number 10 are circled.

The **prime factors** of 10 are **2** and **5**.

10 = 2 x 5

Prime Number

A whole number greater than 1 that has only itself and the number 1 as factors. A number that can be built only one way using tiles. The first 10 prime numbers are 2, 3, 5, 7, 11, 13, 17, 19, 23, and 29.

Prime Number, continued

Example:
17 is a prime number because:
  • it can only be built using 1 row of 17 tiles,
  • 1 x 17 = 17, and
  • its only factors are 1 and 17.

17

1

1 x 17 = 17

Product

The answer to a multiplication problem.

Example:
4 x 8 = 32 **32** is the product.

Progression

A sequence of numbers that has a fixed pattern.

✪ Arithmetic Progression

Each term is the result of adding or subtracting a given number.

Example:
3, 7, 11, 15, 19, . . .
Each number increases by **4** in this arithmetic progression.

✪ Geometric Progression

Each term is obtained by multiplying the preceding term by a given number.

Example:
1, 3, 9, 27, 81, . . .
Each number is multiplied by **3** in this geometric progression.

Quotient

The number that is the answer to a division problem, not including the remainder.

Example:

$$\begin{array}{r} 7\,r3 \\ 6\overline{)45} \\ -42 \\ \hline 3 \end{array}$$

45 ÷ 6 = 7 r 3

7 is the quotient.

Rational Numbers

Numbers that can be written as a ratio. They can be named as fractions or as decimals. These include integers (3, 23), fractions ($\frac{1}{4}$, $\frac{1}{100}$), and terminating or repeating decimals (.25, .333 . . .).

Examples:
.978　　.323232
57　　　1.25 (which equals $\frac{5}{4}$)
−6　　　½

Relationship Symbols

Symbols used to compare the values of two or more numbers or expressions. The most commonly used are =, ≠, >, and <, but there are many more. Also see *Symbols*.

Remainder

The number smaller than the divisor that is left over after the division process has been completed. What is left over after you have put all that you can into equal groups.

Example:
10 ÷ 3 = 3 r 1　　　　　1 is the remainder.

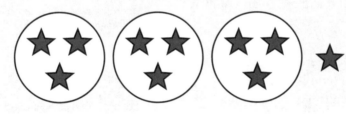

Roman Numerals

Roman letters used to represent numbers. These are usually written in capitals, but they can also be written in lowercase letters. The number is multiplied by 1,000 if there is a bar, or line, over the letter(s).

1 = I	10 = X	19 = XIX
2 = II	11 = XI	20 = XX
3 = III	12 = XII	50 = L
4 = IV	13 = XIII	100 = C
5 = V	14 = XIV	500 = D
6 = VI	15 = XV	1,000 = M
7 = VII	16 = XVI	15,000 = $\overline{\text{XV}}$
8 = VIII	17 = XVII	
9 = IX	18 = XVIII	

Sequence

A set of numbers that is arranged so that there is a pattern. Usually written with the numbers separated by commas.

Example:
2, 7, 4, 9, 6, 11, 8, . . .

Square

To multiply a number by itself.

Example:
$4^2 = 4 \times 4 = 16$

Square Number

A number measured in two dimensions, length and width. To multiply a number by itself. Square numbers are shown with a small 2 above and to the right of the number or unit. Naturally square numbers form a perfect square when built with tiles.

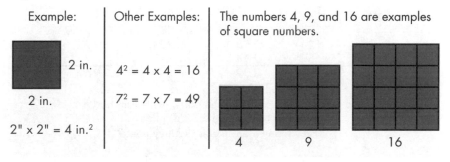

Example:

2 in.

2 in.

2" x 2" = 4 in.²

Other Examples:

$4^2 = 4 \times 4 = 16$

$7^2 = 7 \times 7 = 49$

The numbers 4, 9, and 16 are examples of square numbers.

4   9   16

Square Root

A number that, when squared (multiplied by itself), will produce a given number. The symbol for square root is $\sqrt{\ }$.

★ $\sqrt{49} = +7$ or -7
The square root of 49 is +7 or −7.
★ The principal square root is the positive square root.
$\sqrt{36} = 6$ $\sqrt{100} = 10$

Square Root, continued

Example:
The square root of 9 is 3.

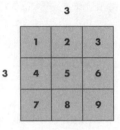

Standard Form

Numbers written in regular number form.

Example:
Three thousand four hundred twenty-two would be written as 3,422.

Subtraction

The process of finding the difference between two numbers.

Examples:

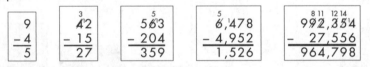

$$\begin{array}{r} 9 \\ -\ 4 \\ \hline 5 \end{array}$$

Fred brought 154 plates for the party, while Kim had 84.
They needed a total of 350 plates.
How many more plates did they need?

154 + 84 = 238 purchased.   350 − 238 = (112) more plates needed.

Subtrahend

The number that is subtracted.

Example:
9 − 6 = 3   **6** is the subtrahend.

Sum

The answer to an addition problem.

Example:
4 + 5 = 9   **9** is the sum.

Triple

To count something three times. Three times as much.

Example:
Triple 4 means the same thing as
4 + 4 + 4 = 12 or 4 x 3 = 12

Twice as Much

Two times as much or two times as many.

Example:
Twice as much as 6 means the same as 6 + 6 = 12 or 6 x 2 = 12

Unequal

Not equal; having a different value; may be different in quantity, size, or amount.

Example:

is not equal to

Whole Number

A number without a fraction or decimal part.

Examples:
1, 34, and 256 are whole numbers.
½, 5 ^{13}/$_{22}$, .45, and 3.7 are not whole numbers.

Zero

The numeral indicating none.

MEASUREMENT

Area

The measurement surface of a region in square units. To find the area, count the squares that can fit inside the object, or multiply the length by the width.

Example:

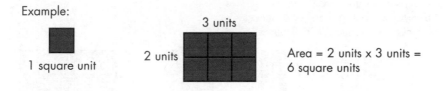

1 square unit

2 units   3 units

Area = 2 units x 3 units = 6 square units

Capacity

The volume of a figure, or the amount of space an object fills. How much something will hold.

Celsius

See *Temperature*.

Centimeter

A unit of metric measurement used to measure length; one centimeter equals 1/100th of a meter; abbreviated cm; also spelled centimetre. One centimeter is about as wide as your little finger is across. See *Metric Measurement–Length*.

Cubed

Having the same measurement in length, width, and height. To raise a number to the third power.

Cubic

Having three dimensions. A cubic solid will have length, width, and height, like a block. Cubic measurements are shown with a small 3 above and to the right of the unit abbreviation.

Example:
Volume = 4^3= 4 x 4 x 4, so
4^3 = 64 in.

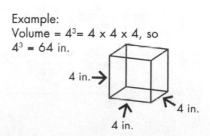

4 in.→

4 in.

4 in.

MEASUREMENT

Cup

A unit of standard measurement used to measure capacity, or volume; often used in cooking; abbreviated c. See *Standard Measurement– Capacity*.

1 cup = 8 ounces
2 cups = 1 pint = 16 ounces
4 cups = 1 quart = 32 ounces
8 cups = 1 half gallon = 64 ounces
16 cups = 1 gallon = 128 ounces

 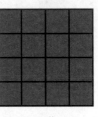

1 cup   1 pint   1 quart   1 half gallon   1 gallon

Currency

A system of money used as a medium of exchange, like coins and paper money. Different countries can have different forms and units of currency. That means that although many countries may have the same names for their currency, they have different values and will look different depending on the country that it comes from. At one time, items such as beads, shells, and furs were all used as currency in different places.

Country	Unit	Subunit
United States	dollar	100 cents
Canada	dollar	100 cents
Great Britain	pound	100 pence
France	Euro	100 cents
Japan	yen	100 sen
Mexico	peso	100 centavos
China	yuan	100 jiao or 100 fen
Russia	ruble	100 kopeks

Decimeter

A unit of metric measurement used to measure length; one decimeter equals 1/10th of a meter; abbreviated dm; also spelled decimetre. One decimeter is a little wider than the width of the widest part of your hand. See *Metric Measurement–Length*.

Degree

A unit of measure for angles. A circle is divided into 360 degrees.

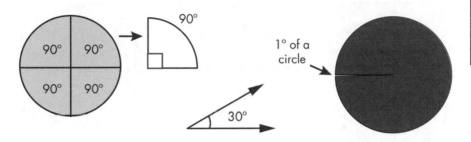

Dimension

Measurement in length, width, depth, or height. The size of something.

✪ Zero-Dimensional

Refers to a specific point or location in space. A point has the property of having zero dimensions. A point will have a single, specific location in one or more dimensions, however, and is usually represented with a dot. It is quite often labeled with a letter.

✪ One-Dimensional

Refers to the characteristic of having only one dimension, like a line, for example. Motion can take place on that line forward and backward, but only on the line. Points on the line could not veer off at a different angle and still be one-dimensional. The points on the same line are called collinear. Each point is at one location, and its location can be measured only with length. Only one number needs to be used to tell its exact location. For example, Point C is at 3 cm.

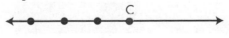

Dimension, continued

✪ Two-Dimensional

Refers to the characteristic of having two dimensions, like a plane figure. Plane figures, such as squares, rectangles, or parallelograms, have the property of being two-dimensional. They can be measured in two directions: length and width. In addition to plane figure shapes, two dimensions can also be found in coordinate graphing and maps, like those that measure latitude and longitude. For plane figures, an area can be determined.

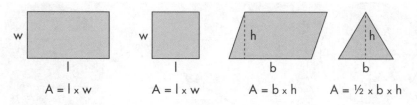

| $A = l \times w$ | $A = l \times w$ | $A = b \times h$ | $A = \frac{1}{2} \times b \times h$ |

✪ Three-Dimensional

Refers to the property of having three dimensions, like a solid figure (also called a space figure). Cubes, rectangular prisms, cones, etc., have the characteristic of being three-dimensional. They can be measured in three directions: length, width, and height (depth, thickness). For space figures, volume can be determined.

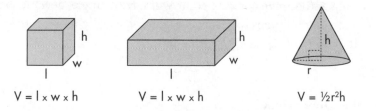

| $V = l \times w \times h$ | $V = l \times w \times h$ | $V = \frac{1}{2}r^2h$ |

✪ Four-Dimensional

The fourth dimension is said to be time itself.

Distance

The length of a straight line between two points. How far it is from one point to another.

Estimate

To find an answer that is close to the exact answer. Your best guess.

Fahrenheit

See *Temperature*.

Foot

A unit of standard measurement used to measure length; 1 foot equals 12 inches; abbreviated ft. See *Standard Measurement–Length*.

Gallon

A unit of standard measurement used to measure capacity, or volume; there are 128 fluid ounces in a gallon; abbreviated gal. See *Standard Measurement–Capacity*.

Gram

A unit of metric measurement used to measure weight; abbreviated g. One gram weighs about as much as a standard paper clip, or about as much as a unit cube of Base-10 blocks. See *Metric Measurement–Mass*.

Half Gallon

A unit of standard measurement used to measure capacity, or volume; there are 64 fluid ounces in a half gallon. See *Standard Measurement–Capacity*.

Height

Height is used to measure vertical lengths. It can be how tall something is, or the distance from the bottom to the top (or top to bottom) of a three-dimensional object. Height can also be how high up something is (i.e., the distance upward from a fixed height).

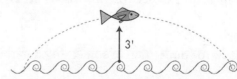
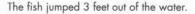

The prism's height is 4".   The fish jumped 3 feet out of the water.

Inch

A unit of standard measurement used to measure length; abbreviated in. One inch is about the width of a quarter. See *Standard Measurement–Length*.

Kilogram

A unit of metric measurement used to measure weight; abbreviated kg. See *Metric Measurement–Mass*.

Kiloliter

A unit of metric measurement used to measure capacity; abbreviated kl; also spelled kilolitre. See *Metric Measurement–Capacity*.

Kilometer

A unit of metric measurement used to measure length; abbreviated km; also spelled kilometre. See *Metric Measurement–Length*.

Length

One-dimensional measurement. The distance from one end to the other end of a line segment. How long something is. When trying to decide which measurement is the length and which is the width, remember that *length* is usually the *longer* of the two.

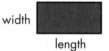

Liter

A unit of metric measurement used to measure capacity; abbreviated L; also spelled litre. See *Metric Measurement–Capacity*.

Measurement

The size or dimension of something determined by measuring.

Measurement, continued
✪ Metric Measurement

Capacity (Volume)

milliliter (ml)	one centicube is a milliliter	1,000 milliliters = 1 liter
liter (L)	1 liter = 1,000 milliliters	
kiloliter (kl)	1 kiloliter = 1,000 liters	

Length

millimeter (mm)   *about as thick as the skinny part of a dime*
10 millimeters = 1 centimeter

centimeter (cm)   *about as wide as your little finger is across*
10 centimeters = 1 decimeter
100 centimeters = 1 meter

View of expanded size metric ruler: 1 centimeter
The little lines in between the "cm" and the "1"
are millimeters.

1 cm

10 mm = 1 cm

cm   1 mm   1

decimeter (dm)   1 decimeter = 10 centimeters
10 decimeters = 1 meter

meter (m)   1 meter = 10 dm = 100 cm = 1,000 mm

kilometer (km)   *used to measure long distances*
1 kilometer = 1,000 meters

Mass

milligram (mg)   1,000 milligrams = 1 gram

gram (g)   *about the mass of a paper clip, or one centicube*
1 gram = 1,000 milligrams
1,000 grams = 1 kilogram

kilogram (kg)   1 kilogram = 1,000 grams

MEASUREMENT

Measurement, continued

✪ **Standard Measurement**

Capacity (Volume)

cup (c)   1 cup = 8 ounces
               2 cups = 1 pint = 16 ounces
               4 cups = 1 quart = 32 ounces
pint (pt)   2 pints = 1 quart = 32 ounces
quart (qt)   4 quarts = 1 gallon = 128 ounces
half gallon   1 half gallon = 2 quarts = 64 ounces
gallon (gal)   1 gallon = 4 quarts = 128 ounces

Length

inch (in. or ")   *about as wide as a quarter*   12 inches = 1 foot
foot (ft or ')   1 foot = 12 inches
                  3 feet = 36 inches = 1 yard
yard (yd)   1 yard = 3 feet = 36 inches
mile (mi)   1 mile = 5,280 feet

View of expanded size standard ruler: 1 inch

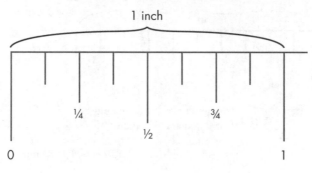

Mass

ounce (oz)   16 ounces = 1 pound
pound (lb)   1 pound = 16 ounces
ton (T)   1 ton = 2,000 pounds

Meter

A unit of metric measurement used to measure length; abbreviated m;
also spelled metre. See *Metric Measurement–Length*.

Metric System of Measurement

The system of measuring that is currently used as the world standard. It is the measuring system used commonly by scientists, and the official unit of measurement for most of the world's nations. Although the metric system is used more often in most places, the standard system of measurement (see p. 42) is still often used in many places and industries. This system uses the following units as a standard of measure:

- Capacity: milliliter, liter, kiloliter
- Length: millimeter, centimeter, decimeter, meter, kilometer
- Mass: milligram, gram, kilogram

See *Metric Measurement*.

Mile

A unit of standard measurement used to measure length; abbreviated mi. See *Standard Measurement–Length*.

Milligram

A unit of standard measurement used to measure weight; abbreviated mg. See *Metric Measurement–Weight*.

Milliliter

A unit of metric measurement used to measure capacity; abbreviated ml; also spelled millilitre. See *Metric Measurement–Capacity*.

Millimeter

A unit of metric measurement used to measure length; abbreviated mm; also spelled millimetre. See *Metric Measurement–Length*.

Money

The standard measure of exchange that is used to buy goods and services, with each unit having a value. The denominations of money used in the United States and Canada are given on pages 38–39.

Money, continued

✪ Penny (coin in U.S. and Canada)

A penny equals one cent.

It takes 100 pennies to make $1.

1 penny = 1 cent (1¢)
5 pennies = 1 nickel (5¢)
10 pennies = 1 dime (10¢)
25 pennies = 1 quarter (25¢)
50 pennies = 1 half-dollar (50¢)
100 pennies = 1 dollar ($1.00)

✪ Nickel (coin in U.S. and Canada)

One nickel equals five cents.

1 nickel = 5 cents (5¢)
2 nickels = 1 dime (10¢)
5 nickels = 1 quarter (25¢)
20 nickels = 1 dollar ($1.00)

✪ Dime (coin in U.S. and Canada)

One dime equals 10 cents.

1 dime = 10 cents (10¢)
5 dimes = 50 cents = 2 quarters (50¢)
10 dimes = 1 dollar ($1.00)

✪ Quarter (coin in U.S. and Canada)

One quarter equals 25 cents.

1 quarter = 25 cents (25¢)
2 quarters = 50 cents (50¢)
4 quarters = 1 dollar ($1.00)

Money, continued

✪ Half-Dollar (coin in U.S.)

One half-dollar equals 50 cents.

1 half-dollar = 50 cents (50¢)
2 half-dollars = 1 dollar ($1.00)

✪ Dollar (paper currency in U.S., coin in Canada)

One dollar equals 100 cents. In the United States, the dollar bill is paper currency; in Canada, the dollar is a coin commonly called a Loonie, in reference to the Loon minted on it. Although the United States has a $2 bill, it is no longer commonly used, and it is rare to see one in circulation. A $2 coin in Canada called a Toonie is in active circulation.

1 dollar = 2 half-dollars
          = 4 quarters
          = 10 dimes
          = 20 nickels
          = 100 pennies

$1 Loonie, Canada $2 Toonie, Canada

Ounce

A unit of standard measurement used to measure weight; abbreviated oz. See *Standard Measurement–Mass*.

MEASUREMENT

Perimeter

The distance around the outside of a figure. To find the perimeter of a rectangular or square figure, find the measurement of each side of the object, and then add the numbers together.

3 units

2 units   2 units

3 units

perimeter = 2 + 3 + 2 + 3 = **10 units**

Pint

A unit of standard measurement used to measure capacity; abbreviated pt. See *Standard Measurement–Capacity*.

Pound

A unit of standard measurement used to measure weight; there are 16 ounces in a pound; abbreviated lb. See *Standard Measurement–Mass*.

Protractor

An instrument in the shape of a semicircle used for drawing and measuring angles in degrees.

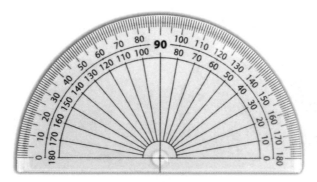

Quart

A unit of standard measurement used to measure capacity; abbreviated qt. See *Standard Measurement–Capacity*.

Rounding

Rewriting a number as its nearest multiple of 10, 100, 1,000, and so on. If the number to the right of the place you are rounding to is 0–4, the number stays the same. If it is 5–9, the number rounds up to the next greater number. The rest of the numbers to the right of the original number become zeros.

Example 1:
Round **3,294** to the nearest thousand.

Look at the number in the place you are rounding; underline it and the number right after it. **3,294**

The number to the right of the 3 is 2, so the 3 will stay the same. The rest of the numbers will change to zeros. Therefore, 3,294 rounds to **3,000** when rounding to the nearest thousand.

Example 2:
Round to the nearest 10

566	$\longrightarrow$	570
562	$\longrightarrow$	560
3,049	$\longrightarrow$	3,050

Round to the nearest 100

566	$\longrightarrow$	600
536	$\longrightarrow$	500
76,824	$\longrightarrow$	76,800

Round to the nearest 10,000

64,340	$\longrightarrow$	60,000
868,473	$\longrightarrow$	870,000
406,299	$\longrightarrow$	410,000

Ruler

A tool used for measuring and drawing straight lines that is usually divided into units and fractional parts of the units, such as inches or centimeters.

Scale

Any instrument that is divided into equal units that can be used to measure. Rulers, thermometers, and weighing devices are examples of scales. Weighing devices are most commonly referred to as scales or balance scales.

Squared

Measuring in two dimensions. A squared figure will be measured for length and width, like a square. Squared measurements are shown with a small 2 above and to the right of the unit abbreviation.

Example:

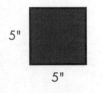

5"

5"

Area = 5^2 = 5 x 5, so 5^2 = 25 in.

Standard System of Measurement

The system of measuring that is currently used in the United States. This system uses the following units as a standard of measure:

- Capacity: cup, pint, quart, gallon
- Length: inch, foot, yard, mile
- Mass: ounce, pound, ton

See *Standard Measurement*.

Surface Area

The combined areas of all surfaces of a three-dimensional figure.

Example 1:
One face of a cube is 3 x 3, which equals 9. There are 6 faces on a cube, so 9 x 6 = 54.

Example 2:
The surface area of a cube with sides equal to 4 is 6 x 4^2, so 6 x 16 = 96.

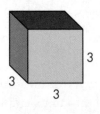

3

3

3

Temperature

The measure of hotness or coldness of an object.

✪ Celsius

Metric, or centigrade, scale of measurement of temperature that is abbreviated with a capital C.

0° C = freezing point of water
100° C = boiling point of water
20° C = normal room temperature

✪ Fahrenheit

Standard scale of measurement of temperature that is abbreviated with a capital F.

32° F = freezing point of water
212° F = boiling point of water
70° F = normal room temperature

Thermometer

An instrument used for measuring temperatures in Celsius, Fahrenheit, or both.

Time

A number that represents a specific interval such as hours, days, or years.

a.m.   The time from 12:00 midnight to noon.
p.m.   The time from 12:00 noon to midnight.

60 seconds = 1 minute	52 weeks = 1 year
60 minutes = 1 hour	10 years = 1 decade
24 hours = 1 day	10 decades = 1 century
7 days = 1 week	100 years = 1 century
365 or 366 days = 1 year	1,000 years = 1 millennium

There are 12 months in each year, each with a set number of days:

Months in the Year	Days in Each Month	Months in the Year	Days in Each Month
January	31	July	31
February	28 (29 in leap years)	August	31
March	31	September	30
April	30	October	31
May	31	November	30
June	30	December	31

MEASUREMENT

Ton

A unit of standard measurement used to measure weight; abbreviated T. See *Standard Measurement–Mass*.

Unit

A standard of measurement such as millimeters, centimeters, inches, feet, meters, yards, miles, ounces, grams, or pounds. Any amount used as a standard for measuring area, length, or volume.

Volume

The amount of space, measured in cubic units, that something takes up. Finding the volume of a space (three-dimensional) figure is often calculated using multiplication.

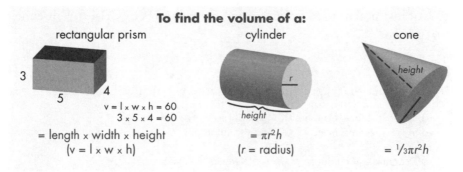

To find the volume of a:

rectangular prism   cylinder   cone

$v = l \times w \times h = 60$
$3 \times 5 \times 4 = 60$
$=$ length $\times$ width $\times$ height
$(v = l \times w \times h)$

$= \pi r^2 h$
$(r = $ radius$)$

$= \frac{1}{3}\pi r^2 h$

Weight

The gravitational pull on an object. The measure of the heaviness of an object. Common units of measure are ounce, pound, gram, kilogram, and ton.

Width

The distance from one side of an object to the other side. How wide something is.

Yard

A unit of standard measurement used to measure length; abbreviated yd. See *Standard Measurement–Length*.

ALGEBRAIC IDEAS

Absolute Value

The value of a number regardless of its sign, denoted by the numeral between two parallel lines. The distance from the origin to that number on a number line.

Example:
$|+3| = 3$ and $|-3| = 3$

Abundant Number

A number in which the sum of its factors is larger than two times the number.

Example:
$12 = 1, 2, 3, 4, 6, 12$
$1 + 2 + 3 + 4 + 6 + 12 = 28$

The sum of the factors is greater than 2×12, so **12** is an abundant number. The sum of the factors is greater than **2n**, where **n** represents the original number.

Additive Inverse

The number that, when added to another number, yields zero.

Example:
$+3 + -3 = 0$
-3 is the additive inverse of $+3$.

Balancing

The process done in equations with an equal sign. An equation is balanced when both sides of the equal sign have the same amount, value, or mass.

Examples:

These equations are balanced.

$7 = 3 + 4 \qquad 6 - 1 = 5$
$24 - 5 = 18 + 1$

This equation is NOT balanced.

$\underbrace{2 + 7}_{9} \neq \underbrace{4 + 4}_{8}$

This equation IS balanced.

$\underbrace{2 + 7}_{9} = \underbrace{4 + 5}_{9}$

Base

The number that is going to be raised to a power using an exponent.

Example:

$$5^3 \leftarrow \text{base}$$

Binomial

A math expression that has two terms. *Bi* refers to two, and *nomial* means part, so a binomial is a polynomial with two terms, or two parts. It is the sum of two monomials. Binomials can have constants, variables, and exponents. They cannot be divided by a variable, have negative exponents, or have fractional exponents.

Examples:

5 + 11	3x + 2y	3x² − 2	5x + 3
2x + 4	6x² + 1	x² − 4x	6x + 3y

Coefficient

The numerical part of an algebraic term. The number used to multiply a variable in algebra.

Examples:

$3x^2$	**3** is the coefficient.
$2y$	**2** is the coefficient.
$5(a + b)$	**5** is the coefficient.
$9x - 3 = 15$	**9** is the coefficient.

Constant

A fixed value or amount. A constant does not have variables; it remains the same.

Example:

$9x - 3 = 15$ **3** and **15** are both constants.

Deficient Number

A number in which the sum of its factors is less than two times the number.

Example:

4 = 1, 2, 4

1 + 2 + 4 = 7

The sum of the factors is less than 2 x 4, so **4** is a deficient number. The sum of the factors is less than **2n**, where **n** represents the original number.

Equation

A number sentence that uses the equal sign. Everything on one side of an equal sign (=) has to equal everything on the other side.

Examples:
$8 + 4 = 12$ $4 \times 5 = 20$
$7 - 3 = 4$ $9 \div 3 = 3$
$35 - 23 = 10 + 2$ $7 + 4 + 3 = 2 \times 7$

A balanced equation; both sides equal the same amount.

$$\underbrace{3 + 4 + 5}_{12} = \underbrace{10 + 2}_{12}$$

Exponent

A small symbol placed above and to the right of a number or letter that shows how many times the base is to be multiplied by itself.

6^4 ← exponent
↑
base

Example:
$6^4 = 6 \times 6 \times 6 \times 6$, so $6^4 = 1{,}296$
$b^3 = b \times b \times b$
$5^7 = 5 \times 5 \times 5 \times 5 \times 5 \times 5 \times 5$, so $5^7 = 78{,}125$
$7^2 = 7 \times 7$, so $7^2 = 49$

There are several rules that can help when solving problems with exponents:

✪ First Power

Any number raised to the first power always equals the base.

Examples:
$7^1 = 7$
$23^1 = 23$

✪ Negative Numbers and Even Powers

If a negative number is raised to an even power, the answer will always be a positive.

Examples:
$-2^4 = 16$
$-5^4 = 625$

✪ Negative Numbers and Odd Powers

If a negative number is raised to an odd power, the answer will always be a negative.

Examples:
$-3^3 = -27$
$-2^5 = -32$

✪ Positive Numbers

If a positive number is raised to a power, the answer will always be positive.

Examples:
$2^3 = 8$
$4^2 = 16$

ALGEBRAIC IDEAS

Exponent, continued

✪ Zero

Any number other than zero raised to the zero power will equal one.

Examples:
$7^0 = 1$
$36^0 = 1$

Exponential Numbers

Numbers that have an exponent. See *Exponent*.

Fibonacci Sequence

A sequence of numbers discovered by Leonardo Pisano, who called himself Fibonacci. In this number sequence, which is found often in nature, each number is the sum of the two numbers that came before it. See *Golden Ratio*.

Example: 1, 1, 2, 3, 5, 8, 13, 21, . . .

Finite Set

A set that has a specific number of members.

Formula

A set of symbols that expresses a mathematical fact or rule. A short way of writing the rule for a specific equation.

Examples:
$a = l \times w$ (area of a square)
$p = 2l + 2w$ (perimeter of a square)
$a = \pi r^2$ (area of a circle)
$c = 2\pi r$ or πd (circumference of a circle)

Formulas, Common

There are many common formulas that can be used to solve math problems.

b = base B = area of base d = diameter h = height l = length
π = pi (3.14 . . .) r = radius s = side w = width

Area
circle: $\pi r^2 = a$
rectangle: $l \times w = a$
square: $s^2 = a$
triangle: $\frac{1}{2}bh = a$

Formulas, Common, continued

Circumference: $c = \pi d$ or $c = 2\pi r$

Perimeter
circle: see *Circumference*, above
rectangle: $2(l + w) = p$
square: $4s = p$
triangle: $a + b + c = p$, where a, b, and c represent each side

Volume
cone: $\frac{1}{3}\pi r^2 h = v$
cube: $s^3 = v$
cylinder: $\pi r^2 h = v$
rectangular or triangular prism: $l \times w \times h = v$ or $bh = v$
pyramid: $\frac{1}{3}bh = v$
sphere: $\frac{4}{3}\pi r^3 = v$

Identity Element

A number that does not change the value of another number when a certain operation is performed.

✪ Addition and Subtraction
0 is the identity element.

Examples:
$0 + 3 = 3$
$7 - 0 = 7$

✪ Multiplication and Division
1 is the identity element.

Examples:
$1 \times 5 = 5$
$8 \div 1 = 8$

Inequality

Not equal. A statement in which one expression is greater than (>), less than (<), or not equal (≠) to another. The symbol for inequality is ≠.

Infinite Set

A set that has an unlimited number of members.

ALGEBRAIC IDEAS

ALGEBRAIC IDEAS

Inverse

An operation that reverses, or undoes, another; the opposite of.

- Operations: Addition and subtraction are inverse operations, as are multiplication and division.
- Opposites: 4 and −4 are inverses; −53 and 53 are inverses.
- Coordinates: (6, −2) and (−2, 6) are inverses.

Invert

To turn upside down, or reverse.

Example:

$\frac{3}{5}$ inverted becomes $\frac{5}{3}$

Monomial

Mono means one, and *nomial* means part, so a monomial is a polynomial with just one term, or one part. Monomials have no negative exponents and no fractional exponents; they cannot be divided by a variable.

Examples:
42
67x
$12x^2$
−34
$−13xy^2$
$25x^2y^2$

Multiplication of Integers

Positive and negative integers can be multiplied using the following rules:

✪ Different Sign

When two integers with different signs [(+, -) or (-, +)] are multiplied, the product is negative.

Examples:
$+6 \times -4 = -24$
$-8 \times +2 = -16$

✪ Same Sign

When two integers with the same sign [(+, +) or (-, -)] are multiplied, the product is positive.

Examples:
$+7 \times +5 = +35$
$-4 \times -3 = +12$

Multiplicative Inverse

See *Reciprocal*.

Negative Integer

A number less than zero. See *Negative Number*.

Negative Number

An amount, or quantity, less than zero. These numbers are written with a negative sign in front of them, such as −5, −26, or −100. On a number line, these are the numbers to the left of zero. Negative numbers are also called negative integers.

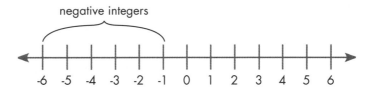

Number Sentence

A statement that involves numbers and their relationship or equality. Number sentences can be true, false, or open.

Examples:
5 × 9 = 45	true
9 + 11 = 4	false
6 + __ = 17	open

Operator

The symbol in an algebra problem that tells what operation to use: +, −, ×, ÷.

Example:
9x − 3 = 15   − is the operator

Origin

In a coordinate system or graph, the point where the axes intersect. The origin (base point) is (0, 0).

ALGEBRAIC IDEAS

Pascal's Triangle

An array of numbers made popular by Blaise Pascal. One use of the triangle is finding the binomial coefficients for expressions like $(x + y)^2$. The triangle has a number pattern in which each number is the sum of the two numbers above it.

```
                    1
                 1     1
              1     2     1
           1     3     3     1
        1     4     6     4     1
     1     5    10    10     5     1
  1     6    15    20    15     6     1
```

Perfect Number

A number in which the sum of its factors equals two times the number.

Example:
6 = 1, 2, 3, 6
1 + 2 + 3 + 6 = 12
The sum of its factors equals 2 x 6, so **6** is a perfect number.

Pi

The ratio between the circumference of a circle and its diameter. Pi's symbol is the 16th letter of the Greek alphabet, so it is written as π. Pi is approximately 3.14159265. . . . It is a nonterminating decimal, which means it goes on forever. Pi is very often rounded to the hundredths place, 3.14, to make it easier to use.

Example:

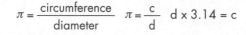

$$\pi = \frac{\text{circumference}}{\text{diameter}} \qquad \pi = \frac{c}{d} \qquad d \times 3.14 = c$$

Polynomial

Poly means many, and *nomial* means part, so polynomial means many terms, or parts, although a polynomial can refer to anything from the sum of one term to the sum of many terms. Polynomials can have constants, variables, and exponents. They cannot be divided by a variable, have negative exponents, or have fractional exponents.

Examples: $4x^2$ $3x^2 + 4x - 7$ $2x^5 - 4x^3 - 8x + 9$

Positive Integer

A number greater than zero. See *Positive Number*.

Positive Number

An amount, or quantity, greater than zero. On a number line, these numbers are to the right of zero. Positive numbers are also called *positive integers*.

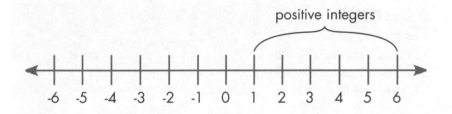

Power

The result of the repeated multiplication of a number by itself. These problems are read as "to the *n*th power," and they are generally written using an exponent.

Examples:
6^4 is read as "6 to the fourth power."
$6^4 = 6 \times 6 \times 6 \times 6 = 1,296$ 1,296 is the fourth power of 6.
$3^2 = 3 \times 3 = 9$ 9 is the second power of 3.
$2^5 = 2 \times 2 \times 2 \times 2 \times 2 = 32$ 32 is the fifth power of 2.

Properties

✪ Associative (Grouping) Property

Changing the grouping of the numbers does not change the sum or product.

Examples:
$(2 \times 3) \times 4 = 24$ $2 \times (3 \times 4) = 24$
$6 \times 4 = 24$ $2 \times 12 = 24$

✪ Commutative (Order) Property

Changing the order of the addends or factors does not change the sum or product.

Examples:
$7 + 3 = 10$ $6 \times 5 = 30$
$3 + 7 = 10$ $5 \times 6 = 30$

ALGEBRAIC IDEAS

Properties, continued

✪ Distributive Property

The product of a number and the sum of two numbers is the same as the sum of the products of the number multiplied by each of the other numbers.

Example:
$3 (4 + 5) = (3 \times 4) + (3 \times 5)$
$3 \times 9 = 12 + 15$
$27 = 27$

✪ One Property

The product of a number and 1 is that number, while the quotient of a number divided by 1 is that number.

Examples:
$7 \times 1 = 7$ $329 \div 1 = 329$

✪ Zero Property

When adding zero to or subtracting zero from a number, the answer is that number. When multiplying a number by zero, the answer is zero.

Examples:
$6 + 0 = 6$
$113 - 0 = 113$
$248 \times 0 = 0$

Real Numbers

The set of rational and irrational numbers. Any number that is positive, negative, or zero.

Significant Digit

A digit that affects the value of a number.

Examples:	
0.73	The zero does not affect the value of this number, so it is not significant.
5.08	The zero holds the tenths place open in this number, and it affects the value of the number. Therefore, it is significant.

Slope

The slope is a number that measures how steep a line is. To find the slope, divide the change in height (y-axis) by the change in horizontal distance (x-axis). A slope can be positive, negative, zero, or undefined. The slope is usually represented with the letter *m*.

Another way to think of it: The x-axis is often called the *run*, while the y-axis is called the *rise*. To calculate the slope, treat it as a fraction and calculate rise over run.

✪ Positive Slope

Lines that go from left to right and go up have a positive slope.

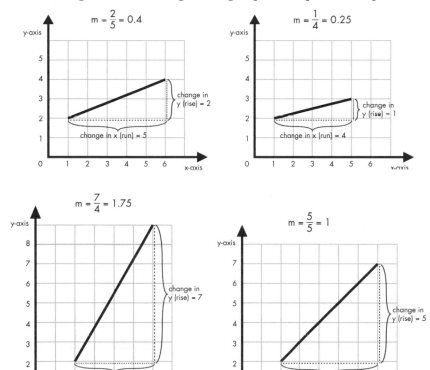

Slope, continued

✪ Negative Slope

Lines that go from left to right and go down have a negative slope.

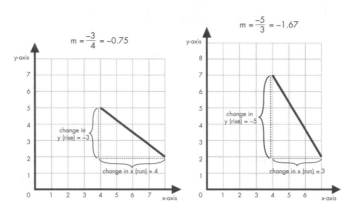

✪ Zero Slope

Lines that go straight across horizontally are said to have no slope, or zero slope.

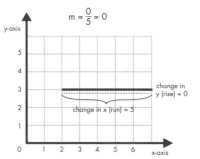

✪ Undefined Slope

Lines that go straight up and down vertically are said to be undefined. This is because the two x-coordinates are exactly the same and have no change, or 0 change. Because you can't divide by zero, the slope is said to be undefined.

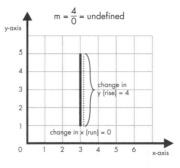

Square

To multiply a number by itself or raise a number to the second power.

Example:
$9^2 = 9 \times 9 = 81$

Square Root

The number that, when squared (multiplied by itself), will produce a given number. The symbol for square root is $\sqrt{\ }$.

Examples: 3 is the square root of 9.   4 is the square root of 16.

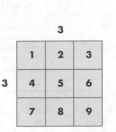

Subset

A set that is part of another set. The symbol for a subset is $\subset$.

Example:
{1, 3, 5, 7} is a subset of {1, 2, 3, 4, 5, 6, 7, 8}
{1, 3, 5, 7} $\subset$ {1, 2, 3, 4, 5, 6, 7, 8}

Symbol

A letter or mark that stands for a quantity, operation, or relationship. A list of common symbols is on page 58.

ALGEBRAIC IDEAS

ALGEBRAIC IDEAS

Symbol, continued

Common Symbols

+	addition	=	equal	¢	penny, cent
…	and so on	!	factorial	%	percent
∠	angle	'	feet	⊥	perpendicular
≈	approximately equal to	≥	greater than or equal to	π	3.14 . . .
∴	averaged with	"	inch	±	plus or minus
⊙	circle	∞	infinity	^	to the power of . . .
≅	congruent to	≠	inequality	→	ray
↔	corresponds to	∩	intersection	≈	similar to
.	decimal	≤	less than or equal to	√	square root
°	degree	—	line segment	⊂	is a subset of
÷	division	×	multiplication	–	subtraction
/	division, fraction	•	multiplication	|	such that . . .
$	dollar	-	negative number	∴	therefore . . .
∈	element of	∉	not an element of	△	triangle
∅	empty set	‖	parallel	∪	union

Trinomial

Tri means three, and *nomial* means part, so a trinomial is a polynomial with three terms, or three parts. It is the sum of three monomials. Trinomials can have constants, variables, and exponents. They cannot be divided by a variable, have negative exponents, or have fractional exponents.

Examples: $5x + 3y^2 - 2$ $x^2 + 7x + 5$ $3x^2 - 2x + 6$

Unknown

The symbol in an equation for which a solution must be found that will make the equation true.

Example:
$3y - 5 = 10$ **y** is the unknown

Variable

A quantity that can have several different values. Anything that changes. A symbol used in an algebra problem to stand for a number that's not known yet. Often the letters "x" or "y" are used. Variables change in different equations.

Example:
$9x - 3 = 15$ **x** is the variable

GEOMETRY

Abscissa

The value of the x-coordinate, or horizontal axis, on a coordinate plane or graph. It is always the first number in an ordered pair.

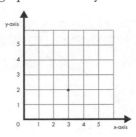

Example:
3, 2   **3** is the abscissa.

Adjacent

To lie or stand near. Adjacent figures are near or beside each other without being separated by other figures.

Adjacent Angles

Two angles that have a common vertex and one common side.

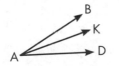

Example:
∠BAK and ∠KAD are adjacent angles.

Adjoining

Sharing a common boundary.

Alternate Exterior Angles

Exterior angles formed by a set of parallel lines intersected by a third line. These angles have the same measure of degrees and are the same size.

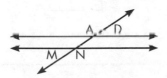

Examples:
∠M and ∠D are alternate exterior angles.
∠A and ∠N are alternate exterior angles.

Alternate Interior Angles

Interior angles formed by a set of parallel lines intersected by a third line. These angles have the same measure of degrees and are the same size.

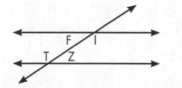

Examples:
∠T and ∠I are alternate interior angles.
∠F and ∠Z are alternate interior angles.

Altitude

See *Height*.

Angle

The figure made by two straight lines meeting at a point (a vertex) or by two rays meeting at a point. The difference between the two lines is measured in degrees.

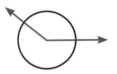

360° = a whole circle
180° = a half (semi) circle
90° = a quarter circle

✪ Acute Angle

An angle smaller than 90 degrees.

✪ Obtuse Angle

An angle larger than 90 degrees but less than 180 degrees.

✪ Right Angle

An angle that has the same shape as the corner of a square. A right angle equals 90 degrees.

✪ Straight Angle

An angle that measures 180 degrees.

GEOMETRY

Angle of Declination

An angle below the horizon, like looking down from the bow of your boat to the anchor on the lake bed. Can also be called the Angle of Depression.

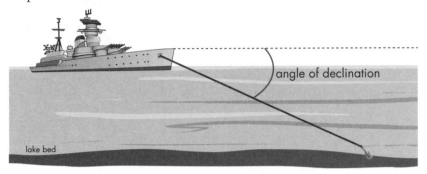

lake bed

angle of declination

Angle of Inclination

Angles above the horizon, like looking up from ground level to the top of something, like a building or a tree. Can also be called the Angle of Elevation.

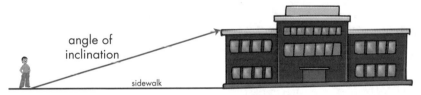

angle of inclination

sidewalk

Apex

An apex is the point (corner, vertex) farthest from the base of a figure. However, it may or may not be a vertex. For example, a cone has an apex, not a vertex. In contrast, a triangle's highest point is usually called a vertex, but can also be called an apex. A prism does not have an apex, only vertices.

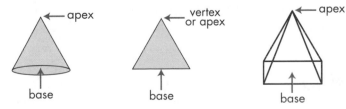

apex

vertex or apex

apex

base　　base　　base

Arc

A part of the circumference of a circle. A part of the edge between any two points on a circle.

✪ Major Arc
An arc that is greater than or equal to 180°.

✪ Minor Arc
An arc that is less than or equal to 180°.

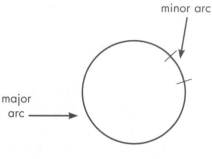

Axis

One of the perpendicular lines used to form a graph. The x-axis (abscissa) is the horizontal axis, and the y-axis (ordinate) is the vertical axis.

Base

The line segment that is the foundation of a geometric figure.

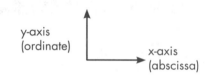

Bisect

To divide into two equal parts.

Bisector

The straight line or ray that bisects (divides) a line or angle into two congruent portions.

Center

A point equally distant from all points on the circumference of a circle or surface of a sphere.

Center Point

See *Center*.

GEOMETRY

Central Angle

An angle whose end points are on the circumference of a circle and whose vertex is at the circle's center point.

central angle →

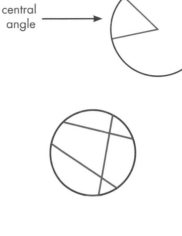

Chord

A line that connects two points on a circle. A diameter is a special kind of chord that passes through the center of the circle.

Circle

A closed curve in which all of the points are the same distance from the point in the center. The distance from the center of the circle to any point on the circle is the radius.

radius

Circumference

The outer boundary, or perimeter, of a circle or circular surface. The distance around the outside of a circle or circular object.

Formula:
C = 3.14 x diameter   (C = π • d)
or
C = 2 x 3.14 x radius   (C = 2 • π • r)

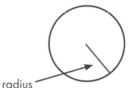

Closed Figure

A two-dimensional figure that does not have an opening to the outside. All of the figure's lines or curves meet to close the shape.

GEOMETRY

Collinear

Lying on the same straight line.

Points A, B, and C are collinear.

Compass

A tool used for drawing circles.

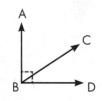

Complementary Angles

Two angles whose sum equals 90°.

Example:
∠ABC and ∠CBD are complementary angles.

Concave

Concave polygons curve inward. In other words, they have at least one angle that points inward toward the interior, like a "cave." One or more corner will be pushed in toward the interior. One or more of its interior angles will be greater than 180°.

Concentric

Sharing a common center.

Cone

A solid figure that has a circular bottom and one flat face.

GEOMETRY

Congruent

Figures that have the same size and shape. The symbol for congruency is ≅.

△ABC ≅ △DEF

Convex

Convex polygons have all of their angles pointing outward. They will have no angles that point inward toward the interior. Their interior angles will be less than 180°.

Convex can also refer to an object that is curved or rounded outward, like a circle or a sphere.

Coordinates

The two numbers in a number pair used to find or define the position of a point or line. Also called a number pair and an ordered pair. The first number in the pair refers to the location on the x-axis, while the second number refers to the location on the y-axis.

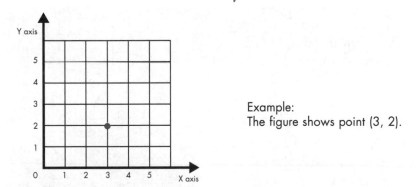

Example:
The figure shows point (3, 2).

Coplanar Lines

Two parallel or intersecting lines that rest in the same plane.

Corner

See *Vertex*.

Corresponding Angles

Pairs of equal angles that are created when parallel lines are intersected by a third line. Four sets of corresponding angles are formed at the intersection. Corresponding angles are the same size in degrees.

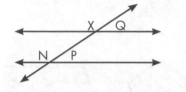

Example:
∠X and ∠N are corresponding angles.
∠Q and ∠P are corresponding angles.

Corresponding Parts

Parts, such as points, sides, or angles, of two congruent figures that have the same position and are the same size.

Example:
Side AC corresponds to DF and ∠A corresponds to ∠D.

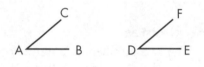

Cube

A special kind of rectangular prism; a three-dimensional figure that has 6 square faces, 8 vertices, and 12 edges.

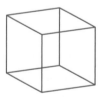

Cuboid

A solid object that is shaped like a box. A cuboid has 6 rectangles for faces. A cuboid is also called a rectangular prism.

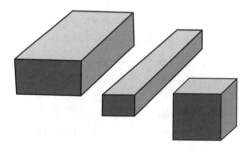

GEOMETRY

Curve

A path that is not straight, but that will show curvature. There are several types of curves, but some common curves include closed curves, open curves, simple curves, and nonsimple curves.

✪ Closed Curve

A curve that is closed because it has no endpoints and completely outlines, or encloses, an area. There will be no open space from which to get inside or outside without crossing a line.

✪ Open Curve

A curve that is open when it has endpoints and leaves part of an area open. There will be an open space from which to get inside or outside without crossing a line.

✪ Simple Curve

A simple curve is a curve that does not cross itself. These can either be open or closed.

✪ Nonsimple Curve

A nonsimple curve is a curve that crosses itself. These can also be either closed or open.

Cylinder

A three-dimensional figure that has two circles for faces.

Decagon

A polygon with 10 sides and 10 angles. Also called a 10-gon.

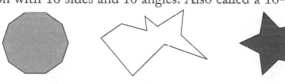

GEOMETRY

Deltoid

See *Kite*.

Diagonal

A line extending in a slanting manner across opposite corners in a polygon.

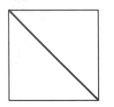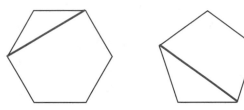

Diameter

A special kind of chord that passes through the center of a circle joining two opposite points. The length of a diameter is equal to two radii. The diameter divides a circle into two equal parts called semicircles.

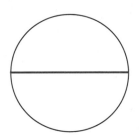

Dimension

The number of basic units used to measure a geometric figure.

- one-dimensional —
- two-dimensional ▪
- three-dimensional ◼

Dodecagon

A polygon with 12 sides and 12 angles. Also called a 12-gon.

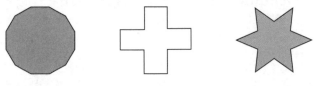

GEOMETRY

Edge

A straight line segment that is the intersection of two faces of a solid figure. The place where faces come together or meet.

Edge

Edge

Edge

Ellipse

An oval. A closed plane curve that has two centers (foci) that define the shape and size of the outer perimeter.

End Point

The point that marks the end of a line segment or ray.

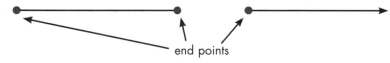

end points

Equiangular

Having all angles equal. A square is equiangular.

Equidistant

The state of being an equal distance from a point so that the lines that connect the points are congruent, or the same length.

Example:

Point A is equidistant from Point S and Point M; SA is congruent to AM.

Equilateral

Having all sides equal.

Exterior

Outside a figure.

GEOMETRY

Exterior Angle

An angle on the outside of a polygon that is formed by the extension of one side and the adjacent side of the polygon.

Face

One of the plane figures that make up a space figure.

Flip

To turn over.

Front View

The view of something from the front.

Golden Ratio

The "golden ratio" is a special number that equals 1.618. It is a ratio found often in nature and has been recognized since the time of the Ancient Greeks as pleasing to the eye.

The Golden Ratio and the Fibonacci Sequence have a special relationship. If you take two consecutive numbers in the Fibonacci Sequence, starting with the number 2, their **ratio** is close to the Golden Ratio.

Example: 0, 1, 1, 2, 3, 5, 8, 13, 21, 34, 55, 89...

2, 3 ➤ 3:2 ➤ 3/2 = 1.5	13, 21 ➤ 21:13 ➤ 21/13 = 1.61
3, 5 ➤ 5:3 ➤ 5/3 = 1.66	21, 34 ➤ 34:21 ➤ 34/21 = 1.61
5, 8 ➤ 8:5 ➤ 8/5 = 1.6	34, 55 ➤ 55:34 ➤ 55/34 = 1.61
8, 13 ➤ 13:8 ➤ 13/8 = 1.62	...and so on

GEOMETRY

Golden Ratio, continued

The Golden Ratio and the Fibonacci Sequence can be found in many examples in nature, including seashells, flowers, tree branches, pine cones, and the human body. They are also found in art and architecture such as the Parthenon, the Great Pyramid, Notre Dame Cathedral, the Mona Lisa, and The Last Supper, to name just a few.

Golden Rectangle

The golden rectangle is a rectangle that uses the golden ratio to find its dimensions. To make a golden rectangle using calculation, multiply the width by the golden ratio (1.618). That will tell you what the length should be to make a golden rectangle.

Example:

A golden rectangle can also be approximated by drawing it out. The steps are numbered below in the diagram.

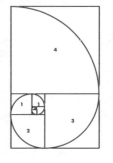

1. Draw two 1-unit squares side by side.
2. Draw a 2-unit square under them.
3. Draw a 3-unit square beside them.
4. Draw a 5-unit square above.

Height

The vertical distance from the base to the highest point. Also called *altitude*.

In a triangle, the height is the perpendicular distance from the vertex to the opposite side.

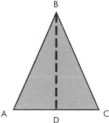

Hemisphere
Half a sphere.

Heptagon
A polygon with seven sides and seven angles. Also called a 7-gon.

Hexagon
A polygon with six sides and six angles. Also called a 6-gon.

Horizontal
Parallel to the horizon and perpendicular to vertical.

Horizontal Symmetry
See *Line Symmetry*.

Hypotenuse
The side of a right triangle that is opposite of the right angle.

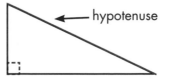

GEOMETRY

Icosagon

A polygon with 20 sides and 20 angles. Also called a 20-gon.

Image

The visual picture, or likeness, of something produced by the reflection from a mirror.

Inscribed Angle

An angle in which all of its points lie on the circle's circumference.

Interior

Inside a figure.

Interior Angle

An angle on the inside of a polygon that is formed by two adjacent sides of the polygon.

Intersecting Lines

Lines that meet at a point.

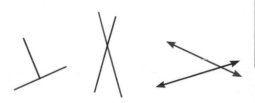

Irregular Polygon

A polygon in which not all of the sides are the same length, and not all angles have the same measure. See *Polygon*.

Kite

A quadrilateral with two pairs of equal sides; each pair shares a vertex. In a kite, the angles of unequal sides are equal, and the diagonals intersect at right angles. Also called a deltoid.

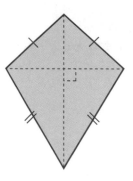

Line

A one-dimensional straight path that is endless in both directions.

Linear

Relating to a straight line; one-dimensional.

Line Segment

A portion (part) of a straight line. There is a point at each end of a line segment, and sometimes the ends will be labeled.

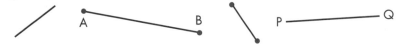

Line Symmetry

✪ Horizontal Symmetry
Parallel to the horizon.

✪ Vertical Symmetry
Perpendicular to the horizon.

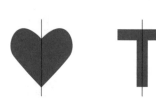

Midpoint

A point that is an equal distance from the two endpoints of a line segment.

midpoint

GEOMETRY

Net

Nets are a two-dimensional representation of the faces of a three-dimensional shape. If a shape figure could be opened and laid out flat, the net is the pattern those faces would take. For some shapes there may be more than one net.

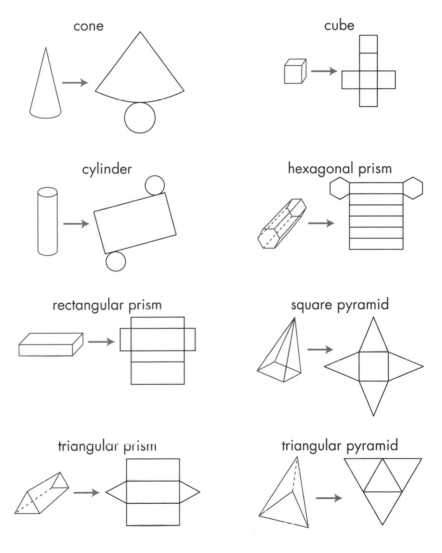

cone

cube

cylinder

hexagonal prism

rectangular prism

square pyramid

triangular prism

triangular pyramid

Nonagon

A polygon with nine sides and nine angles. Also called a 9-gon.

Noncollinear Points

Three points that do not lie in the same straight line.

Number Pair

A pair of numbers that is used to give the location of a point on a graph. Also called coordinates.

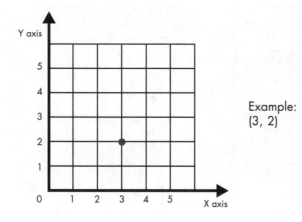

Example:
(3, 2)

Octagon

A polygon with eight sides and eight angles. Also called an 8-gon.

GEOMETRY

Open Figure

A two-dimensional figure that is not closed all the way. It has a place where its lines or curves do not meet.

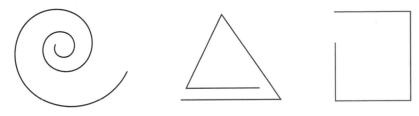

Ordinates

The value of the y-coordinate, or vertical axis, in a coordinate plane, or graph. It is always the second number in an ordered pair. It's how far up or down the point is.

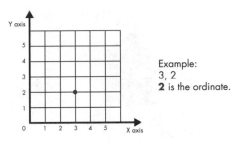

Example:
3, 2
2 is the ordinate.

Origin

In a coordinate system or graph, the point where the axes intersect. The origin (base point) is (0, 0).

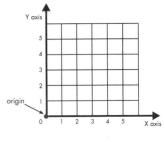

Oval

Although the term "oval" is not strictly a math term, it is commonly used to refer to figures that are elliptical in shape. See *Ellipse*.

Parallel Lines

Lines that do not intersect (cross) and would not ever cross if they were extended. Lines that are equidistant at all points.

GEOMETRY

Parallelogram

A quadrilateral that has two pairs of opposite sides that are both equal and parallel. In a parallelogram, opposite angles are equal (congruent), and adjacent angles are supplementary.

Pentagon

A polygon with five sides and five angles. Also called a 5-gon.

Perimeter

The distance around the outside of a figure. The sum of the length of the sides of a geometric figure.

Example:
perimeter = a + b + c + d

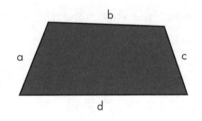

Perpendicular Lines

Lines that intersect to form a right (90°) angle. Lines that form a square corner.

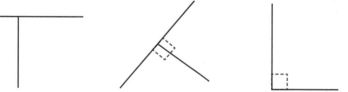

GEOMETRY

Pi

The ratio between the circumference of a circle and its diameter. Pi's symbol is the 16th letter of the Greek alphabet, so it is written as π. Pi is approximately 3.14159265. . . . It is a nonterminating decimal, which means it goes on forever. Pi is very often rounded to the hundredths place, 3.14, to make it easier to use.

Example:

$$\pi = \frac{\text{circumference}}{\text{diameter}} \qquad \pi = \frac{c}{d} \qquad d \times 3.14 = c$$

Plane Figure

A flat shape having two dimensions, length and width, and all points located within the same plane.

Point

A point is a specific location. It has only one position, no size. We represent them as dots so we can see them, but in reality a point doesn't have size. Points are usually given a letter as a name to help identify them from other points.

Examples:

Polygon

A closed figure that is formed entirely by line segments. Examples include pentagons, hexagons, heptagons, octagons, trapezoids, and squares.

✪ Irregular Polygon

Not all of the sides of a figure are the same length, and not all of the angles have the same measure.

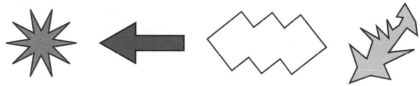

Polygon, continued

✪ Regular Polygon

All of the sides of the figure are the same length, and all of the angles have the same measure.

Polyhedron

A three-dimensional figure with many faces, such as a cube, pyramid, or prism.

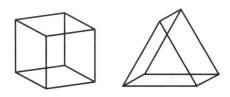

Prism

A solid figure whose ends are parallel, congruent (equal in size and shape) polygons, and whose sides are parallelograms.

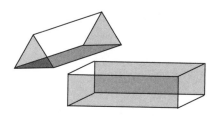

Protractor

An instrument in the shape of a semicircle used for drawing and measuring angles in degrees.

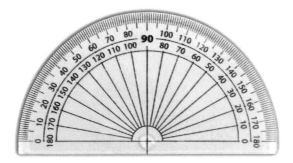

Pyramid

A geometric solid formed by triangles. The faces on a pyramid are triangles that meet at a point (vertex). They can have different shaped bases and are named by the shape of their base.

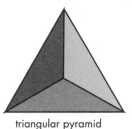
triangular pyramid

square pyramid

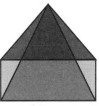
rectangular pyramid

Pythagorean Theorem

A theorem that the sum of the squares of the two sides of a right triangle is equal to the square of the hypotenuse.

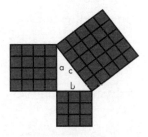

Example:
$$a^2 + b^2 = c^2$$
$$4^2 + 3^2 = 5^2$$
$$16 + 9 = 25$$

Quadrant

A quarter of a plane figure that has been divided by perpendicular lines. Circles can be divided into quadrants. In coordinate geometry, the plane is divided into four quadrants by the x-axis and the y-axis.

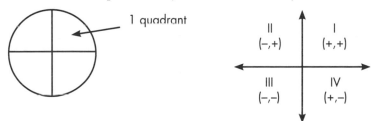

1 quadrant

II (−,+)   I (+,+)

III (−,−)   IV (+,−)

GEOMETRY

Quadrilateral

Any polygon with four sides.

Examples:
square   rectangle
parallelogram   rhomboid
rhombus   trapezoid
trapezium

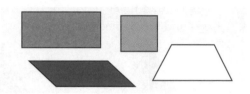

Radius

A straight line that extends from the center of a circle to a point on the circumference of a circle. The radius equals one half of the diameter.

Ray

A straight line that extends from a point forever in one direction.

Rectangle

A quadrilateral and parallelogram that has four right angles and two pairs of opposite sides that are the same length.

Rectangular Prism

A space figure that has rectangles and squares for faces. Rectangular prisms are in the shape of a box, and they have 6 faces, 8 vertices, and 12 edges.

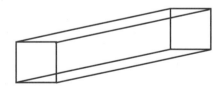

Reflection

The image of an object as seen in a mirror. Reflection is useful in finding symmetry.

GEOMETRY

Regular Polygon

A polygon in which all of the sides and all of the angles are congruent. If a circle is drawn around a regular polygon, all of its vertices will touch the circumference. See *Polygon*.

Rhomboid

A quadrilateral and parallelogram in which opposite sides are parallel, but there are no right angles. Adjacent sides are not equal.

Rhombus

A quadrilateral and parallelogram that has four equal sides.

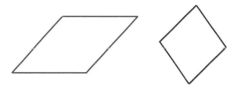

Rotate

To turn or move an object around a point.

Rotation

To turn around a center point.

Rotational Symmetry

A figure is said to have rotational symmetry if it can be turned, or rotated, to fit on itself and still look the same. If it only fits on itself one time (a turn of 360°), it does not have rotational symmetry. Rotational symmetry is named for the number of ways a shape can turn to fit on itself. For example, if it can be turned onto itself exactly three times, it is said to have an Order 3 rotational symmetry.

GEOMETRY

GEOMETRY

Segment
Any of the parts into which something can be separated. A piece or portion of something, such as a line.

Semicircle
A half circle.

Side View
The view of something from the side.

Similar Figures
Figures that have the same shape, but not the same size.

Slant
Also called slant height. For a pyramid, the slant is the distance along the center of a face from the base to the apex. For a cone, the slant is the distance from a point on the base's circumference to the apex.

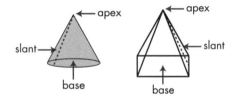

Slide
To move an object or figure without flipping or rotating it.

Slope
The amount of slant or inclination of a line on a coordinate graph.

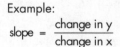

Example:

$$\text{slope} = \frac{\text{change in y}}{\text{change in x}}$$

Space Figure

Another way to describe a three-dimensional shape. Space figures have volume, meaning they take up space.

Sphere

A space figure shaped like a round ball in which every point is equidistant (the same distance) from the center.

Square

A quadrilateral and parallelogram that has four equal sides and four equal 90° angles (right angles). A square is a special type of rectangle.

Supplementary Angles

Two angles whose sum equals 180°.

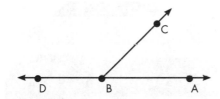

Example:
∠ABC + ∠CBD = 180°

Surface Area

The sum of the areas of all of the flat surfaces on a three-dimensional figure.

Symmetrical

A figure can be considered symmetrical if it has line symmetry, rotational symmetry, or both. Line symmetry is characteristic of a figure that can be folded into two identical halves, or reflected or flipped over a line, yet appears unchanged. Rotational symmetry is the number of ways a shape can be turned, or rotated, to fit on itself and still look the same. If it only fits on itself one time (a turn of 360°), it does not have rotational symmetry. See *Line Symmetry and Rotational Symmetry*.

GEOMETRY

Tangent

A line that touches a figure at one point, but does not intersect it.

Top View

The view of something from the top.

Transversal

A straight line that intersects, or crosses, a set of lines.

transversal

Trapezium

A quadrilateral in which no two sides are parallel.

Trapezoid

A quadrilateral that has exactly one pair of parallel sides.

Triangle

A plane figure with three segments as sides and three angles. The sum of a triangle's angles equals 180°.

✪ Equilateral Triangle

A triangle in which all three sides are the same length and all three angles are 60°.

GEOMETRY

Triangle, continued

✪ Isosceles Triangle

A triangle that has two sides of the same length.

✪ Right Triangle

A triangle that has a right (90°) angle.

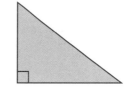

✪ Scalene Triangle

A triangle in which no sides are the same length.

Triangular Prism

A solid figure that has two triangular and three rectangular faces, six vertices, and nine edges.

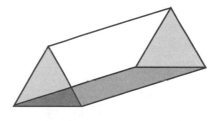

Trisect

To divide into three equal parts.

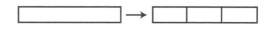

Turn

See *Rotate*.

GEOMETRY

89

Vertex

The point of intersection of rays or line segments. The place where lines or edges meet, or corners. In plane figures, the point opposite the base.

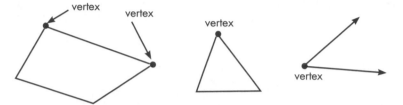

Vertical

Perpendicular to the horizon, or upright.

Vertical Symmetry

See *Line Symmetry*.

Vertically Opposite Angles

Sets of angles that form when two lines intersect. Angles with a common vertex whose sides are extensions of the other angle's sides. Vertical angles lie on opposite sides of the same vertex and are the same size.

Example:
∠A and ∠C are vertically opposite.
∠B and ∠D are vertically opposite.

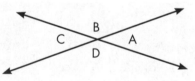

Vertices

The plural of vertex. More than one vertex. See *Vertex*.

DECIMALS, FRACTIONS, PERCENTS, AND RATIOS

Adding Decimals

1. Line up the decimal points so that the place value is in line.
2. Add as normal. Zeros can be added after the decimal point in order to make adding easier, and it won't change the answer.
3. Bring the decimal point straight down into the answer.

Examples:

$$.75 + 2 + 1.674 =$$

$$\begin{array}{r} .750 \\ 2.000 \\ + 1.674 \\ \hline 4.424 \end{array}$$

$$3.5 + .46 =$$

$$\begin{array}{r} 3.50 \\ + .46 \\ \hline 3.96 \end{array}$$

$$.4 + 3 + .27 =$$

$$\begin{array}{r} .40 \\ 3.00 \\ + .27 \\ \hline 3.67 \end{array}$$

Adding Fractions

To add fractions, first look at the denominators.

✪ Same Denominators

1. Leave the denominator the same, and write it in your answer.
2. Add the numerators.
3. Write the sum over the denominator.
4. Reduce (simplify) if needed.

Examples:

$$\frac{7}{12} + \frac{4}{12} = \frac{11}{12} \qquad \frac{3}{7} + \frac{2}{7} = \frac{5}{7} \qquad \frac{4}{8} + \frac{2}{8} = \frac{6}{8} \div \frac{2}{2} = \frac{3}{4}$$

✪ Different Denominators

1. Find a common denominator.
2. Make equivalent fractions.
3. Add the numerators.
4. Write the sum over the common denominator.
5. Reduce (simplify) if needed.

Adding Fractions, continued

✪ Different Denominators, continued

Examples:

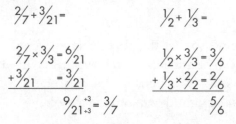

$$\tfrac{2}{7}+\tfrac{3}{21}=$$

$$\tfrac{2}{7}\times\tfrac{3}{3}=\tfrac{6}{21}$$
$$+\tfrac{3}{21}\qquad=\tfrac{3}{21}$$
$$\tfrac{9}{21}{}^{\div3}_{\div3}=\tfrac{3}{7}$$

$$\tfrac{1}{2}+\tfrac{1}{3}=$$

$$\tfrac{1}{2}\times\tfrac{3}{3}=\tfrac{3}{6}$$
$$+\tfrac{1}{3}\times\tfrac{2}{2}=\tfrac{2}{6}$$
$$\tfrac{5}{6}$$

Changing a Decimal to a Fraction

See *Converting Decimals*.

Changing a Decimal to a Percent

See *Converting Decimals*.

Changing a Percent to a Decimal

See *Converting Percents*.

Changing Improper Fractions to Mixed or Whole Numbers

See *Converting Fractions*.

Changing Mixed Numbers to Improper Fractions

See *Converting Fractions*.

Common Denominator

See *Denominator*.

Comparing Decimals

To determine which decimal is larger or smaller, place value must be compared.

1. Line up the decimal points.
2. Compare tenths, then hundredths, and then thousandths.

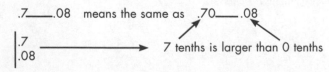

.7____.08 means the same as .70____.08

.7
.08 ————————→ 7 tenths is larger than 0 tenths

Comparing Decimals, continued

1. Line up the decimal points.
   0.41
   0.275

2. Look at place value: 4 tenths is larger than 2 tenths, so **0.41** is larger than **0.275**.

Comparing Fractions

There are several ways to compare fractions.

✪ Method 1: Convert Fractions to Decimals

Write each fraction as a division problem, divide to find the decimals, and then compare the decimal numbers to determine which is larger.

Example:

$$\frac{5}{7} \underline{\quad} \frac{2}{3}$$

```
     .71              .66
  7)4 5.⁴00        3)¹2.¹00
   -4 9             -1 8
    10               20
    -7              -18
     3                2
```

.71 is greater than .66,
so $\frac{5}{7}$ is greater than $\frac{2}{3}$.

✪ Method 2: Cross Multiply

Multiply the numerator of one fraction by the denominator of the other. Repeat the process with the other two numbers, and compare the two products to determine which fraction is larger.

Example:

$$\frac{8}{12} \times \frac{4}{7}$$

7 x 8 = 56
12 x 4 = 48
56 is greater than 48, so 8/12 is greater than 4/7.

✪ Method 3: Find a Common Denominator

Find a common denominator for both fractions, and then compare the two fractions to determine which is larger.

Comparing Fractions, continued
✪ Method 3: Find a Common Denominator, continued

To find a common denominator, multiply or divide both the numerator and denominator of a fraction or fractions by the same number. Sometimes you will only need to adjust one of the fractions.

$$\frac{1}{2} \times \frac{5}{5} = \frac{5}{10} \quad\bigg|\quad \frac{2}{3} \times \frac{2}{2} = \frac{4}{6}$$

$$\frac{3}{5} \times \frac{2}{2} = \frac{6}{10} \quad\bigg|\quad \frac{3}{6}$$

Now that they have a common denominator, they can be compared, added, or subtracted easily.

Complex Fraction

A complex fraction has a mixed or fractional number for its numerator or denominator.

Example:

Converting Decimals

✪ Decimal to Fraction
To change a decimal to a fraction, use place value.

1. Decide whether the decimal represents tenths, hundredths, thousandths, etc.
2. Write the numerical part of the decimal over the appropriate power of 10— over 10 if the decimal was in the tenths place, over 100 if the decimal was in the hundredths place, and so on.
3. Reduce the fraction.

Example:
.05 is 5 hundredths

$$\frac{5}{100} \qquad \frac{5}{100} \div \frac{5}{5} = \frac{1}{20}$$

✪ Decimal to Percent
To change a decimal to a percent, move the decimal point.

1. Move the decimal point two places to the right.
2. Add a percent sign (%).
3. Add zeros for placeholders if necessary.

Converting Decimals, continued
✪ Decimal to Percent, continued

Examples:
.56 = 56%   .489 = 48.9%
.05 = 5%   .3 = 30%

Converting Fractions
✪ Fraction to Decimal

To find the decimal for a fraction: ⅝

1. Divide the numerator by the
    denominator

$$8\overline{)5}$$

2. Add a decimal point and 0's
    to the dividend. Bring the
    decimal point straight up to the
    quotient.

$$8\overline{)5.00}$$

3. Divide as normal; write the
    answer with the decimal point.

$$
\begin{array}{r}
.625 \\
8\overline{)5.00} \\
-48 \\
\hline
20 \\
-16 \\
\hline
40 \\
-40 \\
\hline
0
\end{array}
$$

✪ Improper Fraction to Mixed or Whole Number
To convert an improper fraction to a mixed or whole number, use division.

1. Divide the numerator by the
    denominator.
2. Write the remainder as a
    fraction.

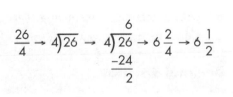

$$\frac{26}{4} \rightarrow 4\overline{)26} \rightarrow 4\overline{)\underset{2}{\overset{6}{26}}} \rightarrow 6\frac{2}{4} \rightarrow 6\frac{1}{2}$$

Converting Fractions, continued

✪ Mixed Number to Improper Fraction

To convert a mixed number to an improper fraction, use multiplication.

1. Multiply the denominator by the whole number.
2. Add the numerator to the answer.
3. Put the answer over the original denominator.

$$5\frac{3}{7} = 5\frac{{}^{+}3}{{}_{\times}7} = \frac{38}{7} \quad \text{or} \quad 5\frac{3}{7} = \frac{(5\times7)+3}{7} = \frac{38}{7}$$

7 x 5 = 35   7 x 5 + 3
35 + 3 = 38   The denominator stays the same.
$^{38}/_{7}$

Converting Percents

✪ Percent to a Decimal

To change a percentage to a decimal, move the decimal point two places to the left. Add zeros as placeholders if necessary.

Examples:
56% = .56   48.9% = .489
5% = .05

Decimal

A special kind of fraction that has a power of 10 (10, 100, 1,000, 10,000, . . .) for a denominator. Decimals are part of a whole. They are written with a decimal point, using place value, instead of as a fraction.

Decimal Fraction

A fraction whose denominator is a power of 10, such as 10, 100, or 1,000.

Examples:
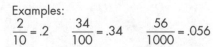

$$\frac{2}{10} = .2 \qquad \frac{34}{100} = .34 \qquad \frac{56}{1000} = .056$$

Decimal Point

A dot written in a number that separates the whole number from the fractional part. The decimal point is read as "and."

Denominator

The number that is written below the line in a fraction. It shows into how many equal pieces the whole has been divided.

Example:

$\dfrac{6}{8}$ ⟵ **8** is the denominator

✪ Common Denominator

A common multiple of the denominators of two or more fractions.

Example:

$^1/_2$ Multiples of 2: 2 4 6 8 **10** 12 14 16 18 **20** 22 . . .

$^3/_5$ Multiples of 5: 5 **10** 15 **20** 25 30 35 40 45 50 55 . . .

10 and 20 are multiples of 2 and 5, so **10** and **20** are common denominators of $^1/_2$ and $^3/_5$.

Using 10 as a common denominator, multiply both the numerator and denominator of one fraction by the number needed to produce a denominator of 10. Repeat for the second fraction. The numbers by which the fractions are multiplied will usually be different for each fraction.

$$\frac{\mathbf{1}}{\mathbf{2}} \times \frac{5}{5} = \frac{5}{10}$$

$$\frac{\mathbf{3}}{\mathbf{5}} \times \frac{2}{2} = \frac{6}{10}$$

Now that the fractions have a common denominator, they can be compared, added, or subtracted easily.

$$\frac{\mathbf{2}}{\mathbf{3}} \times \frac{2}{2} = \frac{4}{6}$$

$$\frac{\mathbf{3}}{\mathbf{6}}$$

Sometimes you will only need to adjust one of the fractions. The fractions now can be compared, added, or subtracted.

Denominator, continued

✪ Lowest Common Denominator (LCD)

The lowest denominator that two or more fractions have in common.

Example:
$^1/_2$ Multiples of 2:   2   4   **6**   8   10   12   14   16 . . .
$^2/_3$ Multiples of 3:   3   **6**   9   12   15   18   21   24 . . .

6 is the lowest common multiple of 2 and 3, so it is the lowest common denominator (LCD) of $^1/_2$ and $^2/_3$.

$$\frac{1}{2} = \frac{3}{6} \quad and \quad \frac{2}{3} = \frac{4}{6}$$

Dividing Decimals

1. Write the problem as normal.
2. Bring the decimal point straight up.
3. Divide as normal.

$$
\begin{array}{r}
0.71 \\
6\overline{)\ 4.26} \\
-4\,2 \\
\hline
06 \\
-\ 6 \\
\hline
0
\end{array}
\quad = 0.71
$$

Dividing Fractions

When fractions are divided, a reciprocal and multiplication must be used. To find a fraction's reciprocal, invert the fraction by writing the numerator on the bottom and the denominator on the top. After the fraction has been inverted, multiply the two fractions together.

✪ To divide regular fractions:

1. Invert the divisor to find the reciprocal.
2. Multiply the numerators.
3. Multiply the denominators.
4. Change the answer to a mixed or whole number.
5. Reduce (simplify) the answer if necessary.

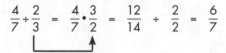

$$\frac{4}{7} \div \frac{2}{3} = \frac{4}{7} \cdot \frac{3}{2} = \frac{12}{14} \div \frac{2}{2} = \frac{6}{7}$$

✪ To divide improper fractions:

1. Invert the divisor.
2. Multiply the numerators.
3. Multiply the denominators.

Dividing Fractions, continued

✪ To divide improper fractions, continued

4. Change the answer to a mixed or whole number.
5. Reduce (simplify) the answer if necessary.

$$\frac{7}{3} \div \frac{8}{4} = \frac{7}{3} \cdot \frac{4}{8} = \frac{28}{24} = 1\frac{4}{24} \div \frac{4}{4} = 1\frac{1}{6}$$

✪ To divide fractions with mixed numbers:

1. Change any mixed numbers to improper fractions.
2. Invert the divisor.
3. Multiply the numerators.
4. Multiply the denominators.
5. Change the answer to a mixed or whole number.
6. Reduce (simplify) the answer if necessary.

$$1\frac{2}{3} \div 2\frac{1}{4} = \frac{5}{3} \div \frac{9}{4} = \frac{5}{3} \cdot \frac{4}{9} = \frac{20}{27}$$

$$3\frac{5}{7} \div 4\frac{2}{3} = \frac{26}{7} \div \frac{14}{3} = \frac{26}{7} \cdot \frac{3}{14} = \frac{78}{98} \div \frac{2}{2} = \frac{39}{49}$$

✪ To divide fractions and whole numbers:

1. Change any whole number to its fractional equivalent.
2. Invert the divisor.
3. Multiply the numerators.
4. Multiply the denominators.
5. Change the answer to a mixed or whole number.
6. Reduce (simplify) the answer if necessary.

$$3 \div \frac{4}{5} = \frac{3}{1} \div \frac{4}{5} = \frac{3}{1} \cdot \frac{5}{4} = \frac{15}{4} = 3\frac{3}{4}$$

$$1\frac{3}{4} \div 6 = \frac{7}{4} \div \frac{6}{1} = \frac{7}{4} \cdot \frac{1}{6} = \frac{7}{24}$$

Eighth

One of eight equal parts.

$^3/_8$ is shown.

Eleventh

One of 11 equal parts.

$^{10}/_{11}$ is shown.

Equivalent Decimals

Decimals that have the same value or name the same amount.

Example:
It helps to think of money: 30 pennies (.30) equals the same amount as 3 dimes (.3).

$$0.30 = 0.3$$

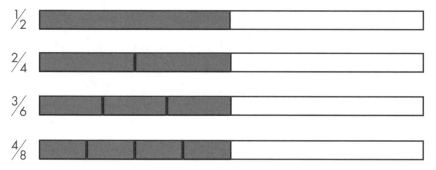

Equivalent Fractions

Fractions that have the same value or name the same amount of a whole.

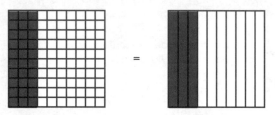

There are several methods to find equivalent fractions.

✪ **Method 1: Multiply or Divide**
Multiply or divide both the numerator and the denominator by the same number.

$$\frac{3}{5} \times \frac{2}{2} = \frac{6}{10} \qquad \frac{4}{7} \times \frac{3}{3} = \frac{12}{21}$$

$$\frac{16}{24} \div \frac{4}{4} = \frac{4}{6} \qquad \frac{9}{18} \div \frac{9}{9} = \frac{1}{2}$$

Equivalent Fractions, continued

✪ Method 2: Use Multiples

List the multiples for the numbers in the numerator and denominator in two separate rows. The numbers in the top row become the numerators in the equivalent fractions, while the numbers in the bottom rows become the denominators.

Example:

$\frac{5}{8} =$	5	10	15	20	25	30	35	40	45
	8	16	24	32	40	48	56	64	72

Fifth

One of five equal parts.

$\frac{1}{5}$ is shown.

Finding a Decimal for a Fraction

See *Converting Fractions*.

Finding a Fraction of a Number

There are two methods for finding a fraction (part) of a number.

✪ Method 1: Draw It Out

Example:

$\frac{3}{5}$ of 20 = 12

Break 20 into 5 groups, then look at 3 of them.

✪ Method 2: Use Division and Multiplication

1. Divide the whole number by the fraction's denominator.
2. Multiply the answer by the numerator.

Examples: $\frac{3}{7}$ of 35

1. Divide the whole number by the denominator to find one fractional part. $35 \div 7 = 5$
2. Multiply the answer by the numerator of the fraction. This finds the number of fractional parts.
3. $\frac{3}{7}$ of 35 = 15   15 is $\frac{3}{7}$ of 35.

Finding a Fraction of a Number, continued
✪ Method 2: Use Division and Multiplication, continued

$\frac{2}{9}$ of 27
- 27 ÷ 9 = 3
- 3 × 2 = 6
- 6 is $\frac{2}{9}$ of 27

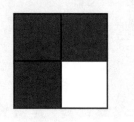

Fourth

One of four equal parts. As a fraction, it is written in simplest terms as ¼. As a decimal, ¼ is shown as .25.

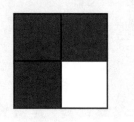

¼ is shown.

Fraction

A number that shows parts of a whole or of a set. The denominator (the number below the line) tells into how many parts the whole has been divided. The numerator (the number above the line) indicates the number of those equal parts being considered.

Example:

$\frac{3}{4}$ numerator (number of parts you have)
denominator (number of parts into which the whole has been divided)

Half

One of two equal parts. As a fraction, it is written in simplest terms as ½. As a decimal, ½ is shown as .50; however, on a calculator it will be seen as .5 without an ending zero.

½ is shown.

Higher Term Fraction

A fraction whose numerator and denominator have a common factor greater than 1.

$\dfrac{2}{4}$ Factors of 2: 1, 2
Factors of 4: 1, 2, 4

2 is a common factor of 2 and 4.

$\dfrac{2}{4}$ is in higher terms and can be reduced because 2 and 4 can both be divided by 2.

$$\dfrac{2}{4} \div \dfrac{2}{2} = \dfrac{1}{2} \qquad \dfrac{4}{12} \div \dfrac{3}{3} = \dfrac{1}{3}$$

Improper Fraction

A fraction in which the numerator is greater than the denominator and represents a value greater than 1. See also *Converting Fractions*.

Lowest Common Denominator (LCD)

See *Denominator*.

Lowest Term Fraction

A fraction whose numerator and denominator have no common factor besides 1. See *Reducing Fractions*.

Examples:
$\frac{1}{3}$ $\frac{2}{5}$
$\frac{3}{7}$ $\frac{11}{24}$

Mixed Number

A number that has both a whole number part and a fractional part, such as $2\frac{1}{3}$. Mixed numbers represent values greater than 1. See also *Converting Fractions*.

$$3\tfrac{2}{3} = \tfrac{11}{3}$$

mixed number   improper fraction

Multiplying Decimals

1. Write and solve the problem as normal.
2. Count the total number of places after each decimal in the numbers being multiplied.
3. Position the decimal the same number of places in the answer.

Multiplying Decimals, continued

```
 7.56  ──▶  .56    2 places to the right of the decimal
×1.2   ──▶  .2     1 place to the right of the decimal
 1512             over 3 places to the left in the answer
+7560
─────
 9.072
```

Multiplying Fractions

The steps taken to multiply fractions depends on the type of fraction in the problem.

✪ To multiply regular fractions:

1. Multiply the numerators.
2. Multiply the denominators.
3. Reduce (simplify) the answer if necessary.

$$\frac{2}{3} \cdot \frac{4}{5} = \frac{8}{15} \qquad \frac{5}{6} \cdot \frac{2}{3} = \frac{10}{18} \div \frac{2}{2} = \frac{5}{9}$$

✪ To multiply improper fractions:

1. Multiply the numerators.
2. Multiply the denominators.
3. Change the answer to a mixed or whole number.
4. Reduce (simplify) the answer if necessary.

$$\frac{4}{3} \cdot \frac{7}{2} = \frac{28}{6} = 4\frac{4}{6} \div \frac{2}{2} = 4\frac{2}{3}$$

✪ To multiply fractions with mixed numbers:

1. Change any mixed numbers to improper fractions.
2. Multiply the numerators.
3. Multiply the denominators.
4. Change the answer to a mixed or whole number.
5. Reduce (simplify) the answer if necessary.

$$3\frac{1}{2} \cdot 2\frac{1}{3} = \frac{7}{2} \cdot \frac{7}{3} = \frac{49}{6} = 8\frac{1}{6}$$

$$1\frac{3}{4} \cdot 1\frac{1}{5} = \frac{7}{4} \cdot \frac{6}{5} = \frac{42}{20} = 2\frac{2}{20} \div \frac{2}{2} = 2\frac{1}{10}$$

Multiplying Fractions, continued

✪ To multiply fractions with whole numbers:

1. Change any whole number to its fractional equivalent.
2. Multiply the numerators.
3. Multiply the denominators.
4. Change the answer to a mixed or whole number.
5. Reduce (simplify) the answer if necessary.

$$3 \cdot 2\frac{1}{3} = \frac{3}{1} \cdot \frac{7}{3} = \frac{21}{3} = 7$$

$$1\frac{3}{4} \cdot 6 = \frac{7}{4} \cdot \frac{6}{1} = \frac{42}{4} = 10\frac{2}{4} \div \frac{2}{2} = 10\frac{1}{2}$$

Ninth

One of nine equal parts.

$^4/_9$ is shown.

Numerator

The number that is written above the line in a fraction. It tells how many parts of the whole are being considered.

Example:

$\frac{6}{8}$ ⟵ **6** is the numerator

Percent (%)

One-hundredth or 1 out of 100 parts. A fractional number with a denominator of 100.

Example:
20% is equal to 20 out of 100.

1. To find a percent, write the number as a fraction.
2. Divide the numerator by the denominator.
3. Multiply the answer by 100.

Percent (%), continued

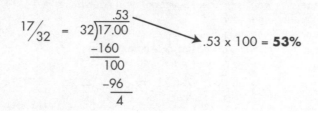

I have 17 out of 32. What percent of the whole is that?

$$\frac{17}{32} = 32\overline{)17.00} \qquad .53 \times 100 = \mathbf{53\%}$$

Place Value

The value given to a digit because of the place it has in the numeral. In decimal numbers, all places are fractions with denominators that are powers of 10, such as 10, 100, and 1,000.

Examples:

$$.5 = \frac{5}{10} \qquad .56 = \frac{56}{100} \qquad .561 = \frac{561}{1,000} \qquad .5617 = \frac{5,617}{10,000}$$

Proper Fraction

A fraction in which the numerator is smaller than the denominator. Proper fractions have a value less than 1.

Examples:
$$\frac{6}{7} \qquad \frac{2}{3}$$

Proportion

An equation that shows that two fractions are equal. These can be written in two ways.

Examples:
$$\frac{1}{2} = \frac{2}{4} \qquad \text{or} \qquad 1:2::2:4$$

Ratio

A comparison of two numbers by division. Ratios are commonly written as a fraction, although they may be written in other ways. The order in which the numbers are written is important: 1:4 is not the same as 4:1.

Examples:
$$\frac{3}{4} \qquad \frac{3}{4} \qquad 3:4 \qquad 3 \text{ of } 4$$

Reciprocal

A number that gives a product of 1 when multiplied by the original number. To find the reciprocal of a number, switch the denominator and the numerator.

Examples:

$$\frac{4}{3} \text{ is the reciprocal of } \frac{3}{4} \text{ because } \frac{4}{3} \times \frac{3}{4} = \frac{12}{12} = 1$$

$$\frac{1}{5} \text{ is the reciprocal of } 5 \text{ because } \frac{1}{5} \times \frac{5}{1} = \frac{5}{5} = 1$$

Reducing Fractions

Reducing fractions is also commonly called simplifying and finding the lowest terms. Regardless of which term is used, to reduce a fraction one must find a factor of both numbers. There are two common methods to reduce (simplify) a fraction to its lowest terms.

✪ Method 1: Use Common Factors

Find the greatest common factor of the numerator and denominator, and then divide both numbers by the factor.

Example:
1, 3, 5, and 15 are common factors of 15 and 45. The greatest common factor is **15**, so divide the numerator and denominator by 15.

$$\frac{15}{45} \div \frac{15}{15} = \frac{1}{3}$$

$\frac{15}{45}$ in lowest terms is $\frac{1}{3}$.

✪ Method 2: Use Prime Factorizations

1. Write the prime factors of each number next to the numerator and denominator.
2. Leave both of the ones alone, but cross off any other factors they have in common.
3. Multiply the numbers on each row to produce a new fraction.
4. The fraction is now in lowest terms.

Reducing Fractions, continued
✪ Method 2: Use Prime Factorizations, continued

$$\frac{14}{26} = \frac{1,\cancel{2},7}{1,\cancel{2},13} = \frac{1\times7}{1\times13} = \frac{7}{13}$$

$$\frac{6}{8} = \frac{1,\cancel{2},3}{1,\cancel{2},2,2} = \frac{1\times3}{1\times2\times2} = \frac{3}{4}$$

Repeating Decimal
A decimal in which one digit, or a series of digits, is repeated over and over again, such as .3333 . . . or .212121. . . . Repeating decimals can be shown in the answer to a problem by using a bar over the first repeating series, such as $.\overline{3}$ or $.7\overline{63}$.

Seventh
One of seven equal parts.

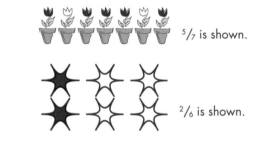

$^5/_7$ is shown.

Sixth
One of six equal parts.

$^2/_6$ is shown.

Subtracting Decimals
1. Line up the decimal points so that the place value is in line.
2. Subtract as normal. Zeros can be added after the decimal point in order to make subtracting easier, and it won't change the answer.
3. Bring the decimal point straight down into the answer.

$$45.9 - 2.53 = \longrightarrow \begin{array}{r} \overset{8\ 10}{45.\cancel{9}0} \\ -2.53 \\ \hline 43.37 \end{array}$$

Subtracting Fractions
To subtract fractions, first look at the denominators.

Subtracting Fractions, continued

✪ Same Denominators

1. Leave the denominator the same, and write it in your answer.
2. Subtract the numerators.
3. Write the difference over the denominator.
4. Reduce (simplify) if needed.

$$\frac{7}{12} - \frac{4}{12} = \frac{3}{12} \div \frac{3}{3} = \frac{1}{4} \qquad \frac{3}{7} - \frac{2}{7} = \frac{1}{7}$$

✪ Different Denominators

1. Find a common denominator.
2. Make equivalent fractions.
3. Subtract the numerators.
4. Write the answer over the denominator.
5. Reduce (simplify) if needed.

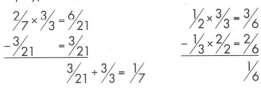

$$\frac{2}{7} \times \frac{3}{3} = \frac{6}{21} \qquad\qquad \frac{1}{2} \times \frac{3}{3} = \frac{3}{6}$$
$$-\frac{3}{21} \quad = \frac{3}{21} \qquad\qquad -\frac{1}{3} \times \frac{2}{2} = \frac{2}{6}$$
$$\frac{3}{21} \div \frac{3}{3} = \frac{1}{7} \qquad\qquad \frac{1}{6}$$

Tenth

One of 10 equal parts.

$^1/_{10}$ is shown.

Terminating Decimal

A nonrepeating decimal with a limited and fixed number of digits.

Examples:
7.25
5.21
8.36

Third

One of three equal parts.

$^2/_3$ is shown.

Twelfth

One of 12 equal parts.

$^5/_{12}$ is shown.

STATISTICS AND PROBABILITY

Average

A number that represents the middle or most normal of a set of numbers. Also called the mean or arithmetic mean.

To find the average (mean):
1. Add all of the numbers together.
2. Divide by the number of items that were added together.

Examples:
3, 5, 5, 11
3 + 5 + 5 + 11 = 24   Four numbers were added, so divide 24 by 4.
24 ÷ 4 = 6   The average (mean) is **6**.

6, 8, 14, 11, 7

$$\frac{6 + 8 + 14 + 11 + 7}{5} = \frac{46}{5}$$

As 46 ÷ 5 = 9 with a remainder of 1, the average (mean) is about **9**.

Axes

Plural of axis.

Axis

One of the perpendicular lines that is used to form a graph. The x-axis (abscissa) is the horizontal axis, and the y-axis (ordinate) is the vertical axis. Together these form the basis of a coordinate plane, as in a coordinate graph.

Coordinate Graphing

A method that uses ordered pairs plotted on axis lines to locate specific points in a two-dimensional plane. Using coordinates can be used for many things, including finding a position on a grid, for mapping, or for plotting a route. See *Geometry—Coordinates*.

✪ 1-Quadrant Coordinate Graphing

1-quadrant graphing uses one quadrant, positive/positive, of the coordinate plane to plot a particular location.

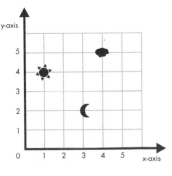

Example: At which point can the sun be found?
(*1, 4*)

STATISTICS AND PROBABILITY

Coordinate Graphing, continued

✪ 4-Quadrant Coordinate Graphing

4-quadrant graphing uses all four quadrants of the coordinate plane to plot a particular location.

Example:
1. Which shape can be found at 1, −5? (*heart*)
2. What is the location of the green rhombus? (*−2, −3*)
3. The location of the purple triangle can be plotted at which coordinates? (*−2, 3*)

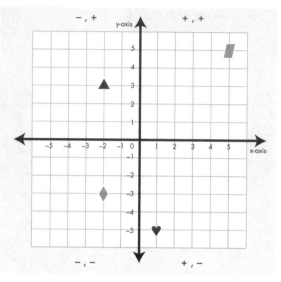

Data

Facts or figures from which conclusions can be formed. Factual information.

Dependent Event

An event whose outcome is affected by another event's outcome.

Event

Something that happens. The set of results or outcomes.

Extrapolate

To estimate a value beyond the known range of data by extending the known relationship or number pattern. To draw a conclusion based on known data.

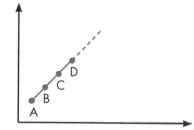

Frequency

How often something happens in a given time. The number of times an event, action, value, or characteristic occurs.

Function Machines

See *Function Table*.

Function Table

A table that shows possible outcomes of a rule, or function. The function relates the input to the output. Function tables can be used to organize data, which can then be plotted into a graph. Function tables are also sometimes called input and output tables or function machines.

Input (x)	Output (y)
1	3
3	6
8	11
12	15
15	
21	
Rule: + 3	

Input (x)	Output (y)
6	60
7	70
10	100
13	
16	
20	
Rule: x 10	

Input (x)	Output (y)
10	5
22	11
4	2
8	4
28	
50	
Rule: ÷ 2	

Input (x)	Output (y)
1	7
2	12
3	17
4	
5	
20	
Function: $y = 5x + 2$	

Graph

A picture that shows information in an organized way. To be complete, a graph needs a title, subtitle, labeled axes, and key (when appropriate).

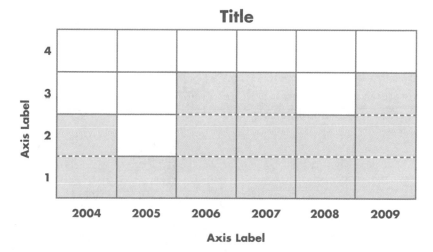

Graph, continued

✪ Bar Graph
A graph that shows information using bars.

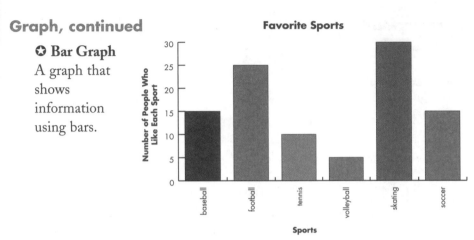

Favorite Sports

✪ Circle Graph (Pie Graph)
A graph that shows all data as a percentage or part of a circle.

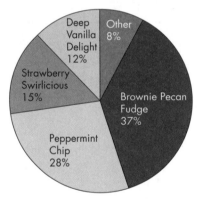

Favorite Flavors of Ice Cream

- Deep Vanilla Delight 12%
- Other 8%
- Strawberry Swirlicious 15%
- Brownie Pecan Fudge 37%
- Peppermint Chip 28%

✪ Glyph
A type of pictograph that uses symbols to represent information. These are used to collect and interpret data.

Key

Eyes:
- Winter is your favorite season: two black eyes
- Winter is OK: one black and one closed eye
- You prefer another season: two closed eyes

Mouth:
- Prefer to go sledding: mouth drawn as smile
- Prefer to play hockey: mouth drawn as circle

Tie:
- Will watch part of the winter Olympics: striped
- Won't watch the winter Olympics: solid

114

Graph, continued

✪ Histogram

A special kind of bar graph that shows how frequently data occurs. The data are usually collected in a frequency table and then put into graph form. In a histogram, the adjacent bars are touching.

Total Number of Students by Age in Our School

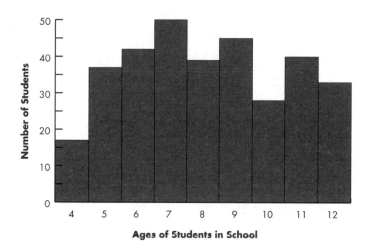

✪ Line Graph

A graph that shows information using lines. These are useful for comparing two or more things.

Amount of Candy Based on Bag Size

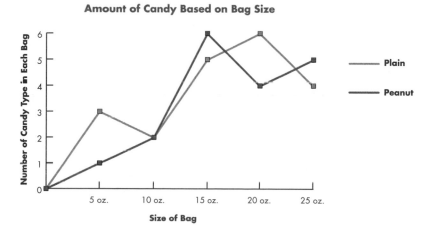

Graph, continued

✪ Picture Graph

A graph that uses pictures to show quantities.

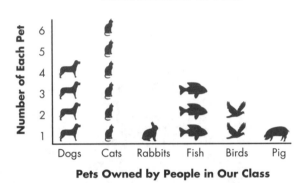

Total Number of Pets

Pets Owned by People in Our Class

Independent Event

An event whose outcome does not affect the outcome of other events.

Input and Output Tables

See *Function Table*.

Interpolate

To estimate a value that is between two known values on a graph.

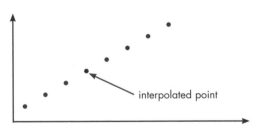

interpolated point

Interval

The amount of space or time between two things or events. The set of numbers between two given numbers or points.

Line Plot

A line plot is a method for organizing data along a number line; it is used to show frequency. Often an "x" or other mark is used to represent each bit of data.

Line Plot, continued

Example:
Mrs. Fitzgerald's class observed the number of birds that visited the feeding station outside their window for 3 weeks. The numbers of birds they saw each day was recorded as follows: 0, 0, 1, 1, 1, 2, 2, 4, 4, 6, 6, 6, 7, 7, 8, 8, 8, 8, 8, 8, 9.

Possible questions:
1. How many days did the class see more than 7 birds at the station? (*7 days— they saw 8 birds 6 of the days, and 9 birds one day*)
2. What fractional number of days during the 21-day observation were no birds seen at the feeder? (*2/21*)
3. There is no mark at 3 on the number line. What does this mean? (*That there was no day during the observation in which exactly 3 birds were seen*)
4. How many days were exactly 4 birds seen at the feeder? (*2*)

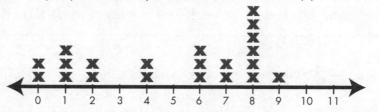

Number of birds seen each day at the feeding station during 21 days of observation.

Mean

The average value of a set of numbers.

To find the mean (average):
1. Add all of the numbers together.
2. Divide by the number of items that were added together.

Examples:
7, 9, 3, 14
$7 + 9 + 3 + 14 = 33$ Four numbers were added, so divide 33 by 4.

$33 \div 4 = 8 \text{ r } 1$ The mean (average) is about **8**.

3, 9, 11, 13, 14
$\dfrac{3+9+11+13+14}{5} = \dfrac{50}{5} = 10$ The mean (average) is **10**.

Median

The number that would fall in the middle if the results were arranged in order from least to greatest (smallest to largest).

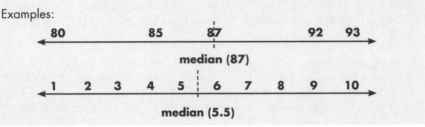

Mode

The number that occurs most frequently in a set of information. When collecting data or information, it's the number of which there is the most.

Example:
5, 6, 7, 7, 9, 11   **7** is the mode.

Odds

The chances, written numerically, that something will or will not happen. These are written as ratios that compare the likelihood of events.

✪ Odds Against

The likelihood that something won't happen.

$$\frac{\text{number of chances against}}{\text{number of chances for}}$$

✪ Odds in Favor

The likelihood that something will happen.

$$\frac{\text{number of chances for}}{\text{number of chances against}}$$

Outcome

A possible result given a set of circumstances.

Percent (%)

One-hundredth or 1 out of 100 parts. A fractional number with a denominator of 100.

Example:
15% means $\frac{15}{100}$ or 0.15

Probability
The chance that something will or will not happen.

Random
All items in the set of information or data have an equal chance of happening or not happening with a certain frequency.

Random Sample
A small portion of a larger population that is selected in such a way that all selections have an equal probability of being chosen. The sample is used as a good representation of the whole population.

Range
The difference between the smallest number and the largest number in the sample.

Examples:
- If the lowest number in the sample is 13 and the highest number is 47, the range is the difference between the two. The range is 47 − 13 = **34**.
- {3, 15, 18, 27, 39}   The range is 39 − 3 = **36**.

Ratio
A comparison of two numbers by division. Ratios are commonly written as a fraction, although they may be written in other ways. The order in which the numbers are written is important; 1:4 is not the same as 4:1.

Examples:
1 to 2   1:2   ½

Sample
A part of something used to represent the whole group. Samples can be used to make predictions about the larger group.

Slope
See *Algebraic Ideas: Slope* (p. 55).

Statistics
Numerical facts or data that can be put together or tabulated to present information about a given subject.

Stem-and-Leaf Plot

A method of categorizing numerical data so that the shape of the distribution easily can be seen. A way of looking at the range of data and its frequency.

Example:
Ages of people in the family:

11	15		
23	24	29	29
31	38	38	
44	47		
56	57		

tens	ones
1	1 5
2	3 4 9 9
3	1 8 8
4	4 7
5	6 7

Survey

A way to gather data or opinions from a sample.

Favorite Lunch Choices at School

Pizza									
Hot Dogs					
Hamburgers			
Chicken Nuggets								

Tally Marks

A set of five lines used to keep track of the number of something when counting. In the United States, Canada, and European countries, these are written as four vertical lines crossed by a diagonal line.

In Asian countries and elsewhere, this mark is shown as the tally symbol.

PROBLEM SOLVING

Algorithm

Any special method of solving a problem.

Attribute

A characteristic, property, or quality of something that is useful in classifying.

Characteristic

A quality, attribute, or property of something that is useful in classifying.

Classify

To arrange or group something into categories according to some rule or common characteristic.

Combination

Any arrangement of elements with no consideration for the order of the elements.

Examples:
- The combinations of the letters A, B, C, and D, taken three at a time, are ABC, ABD, ACD, and BCD.
- The combinations of the letters A, B, C, and D, taken two at a time, are AB, AC, AD, BC, BD, and CD.

Disjoint Sets

Sets that have no members in common.

Example:
$Z = \{p, q, r\}$
$Y = \{d, e, f\}$
$Z \cap Y = \emptyset$

Elements

The things in a set.

Examples:
Set of positive odd numbers between 0 and 10: $\{1, 3, 5, 7, 9\}$
1, 3, 5, 7, 9 are all elements of this set.

$F = \{p, q, r, s\}$
Set F contains the elements p, q, r, and s.

Empty Set

A set that has no elements, shown by using the symbol ∅.

Estimate

To do quick mental calculations (often using rounding) to get an approximate answer.

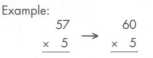

Example:

The answer should be around 300.

Information

✪ Given Information

The information presented in the problem.

✪ Extraneous Information

Information in the problem that is not necessary or relevant to solve it. Extra information.

✪ Necessary Information

Information in the problem that must be used to solve the problem.

Intersection

A set of elements that is common to two sets, shown by the symbol ∩.

Examples:
{2, 4, 6, 8, 12} ∩ {3, 6, 9, 12, 15} = {6, 12}

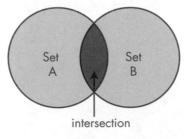

Inverse

The opposite.

Example:
Multiplication is the inverse of division.

Mapping

An operation that matches the members of one set with the members of another set in such a way that the pairs are uniquely paired.

Example:

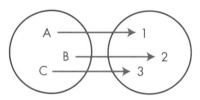

Set 1		Set 2
4	→	7
7	→	10
12	→	15
22	→	25

In this relationship, 12 maps to 15, and 15 is the image of 12.

One-to-One Correspondence

A matching of every element in one set to a unique element in another set.

Pattern

A regular event, happening, or arrangement of numbers, objects, or occurrences.

Permutation

Any of the different ordered combinations possible with a given set of elements.

Example:
The permutations of the numbers 1, 2, and 3 are:
{1, 2, 3} {1, 3, 2} {2, 1, 3} {2, 3, 1} {3, 1, 2} {3, 2, 1}

Property

A characteristic, attribute, or quality of something that is useful in classifying.

Rule

A method used for solving a problem.

PROBLEM SOLVING

Set

A group of things that share some quality in common. A collection or group of numbers or other objects that follow a pattern or rule, have a common characteristic, or are the solutions to a problem. Sets are shown with the use of braces { }. The things that make up a set are called its elements. Sets are usually labelled with capital letters.

Examples:

{2, 4, 6, 8}   {10, 20, 30, 40, . . .}

{crab, lobster, shrimp, barnacle}   {1/2, 2/4, 3/6, 4/8, . . .}

H = {Cinco de Mayo, Mother's Day, Memorial Day} H = {Holidays in May}

A = {dog, cat, fish, bird, turtle}

bird ∈ A means bird **is an element of** set A

D = {c, d, m, a, r)

r ∈ D means r **is an element of** set D

Steps for Successful Problem Solving

1. Read the problem.
2. Find the question asked or problem to be solved.
3. Decide on a problem-solving strategy.
4. Solve using a problem-solving strategy.
5. Reread the problem and check your work to make sure you answered the question correctly.

Strategy

A plan of action used to solve a problem. There are many different strategies that can be used to solve problems.

Examples:

- Act out or use objects.
- Brainstorm for multiple answers.
- Classify.
- Draw a picture.
- Eliminate possibilities.
- Guess and check (also called trial and error).
- Make a simple problem.
- Make an organized list.
- Use a pattern.
- Use logical reasoning.
- Use multiple steps.
- Use or make a table, chart, or diagram.
- Work backward.

Subset

A set that is part of another set. It is shown with the symbol ⊂.

Example:
{1, 3, 5, 7} is a subset of {1, 2, 3, 4, 5, 6, 7, 8}
{1, 3, 5, 7} ⊂ {1, 2, 3, 4, 5, 6, 7, 8}

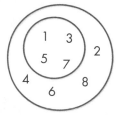

Table

A systematic arrangement of data.

Union

A set of elements, shown by using the symbol ∪, that is the sum of all of the elements in one set and all of the elements in another set.

Examples:
{1, 3, 5, 6} ∪ {2, 4, 6} = {1, 2, 3, 4, 5, 6}

J = {red, yellow, orange}
M = {blue, green, violet}
J ∪ M = {red, yellow, orange, blue, green, violet}

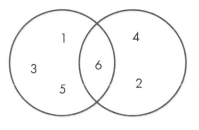

Venn Diagram

Diagrams in which intersecting circles are used to represent different sets of elements. A way to show similarities and differences and compare information.

Examples:

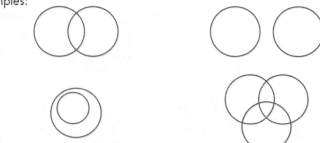

QUICK REFERENCE GUIDES

QUICK REFERENCE GUIDE: DECIMALS

Adding Decimals

1. Line up the decimal points so that the place value is in line.
2. Add as normal. Zeros can be added after the decimal point in order to make adding easier, and it won't change the answer.
3. Bring the decimal point straight down into the answer.

5 + .34 + 2.738 =	.83 + 4.2 =	9 + 6 + .34 =
5.000	.83	.90
.340	+ 4.20	6.00
+ 2.738	5.03	+ .34
8.078		7.24

Comparing Decimals

To determine which decimal is larger or smaller, place value must be compared.

1. Line up the decimal points.
2. Compare tenths, then hundredths, and then thousandths.

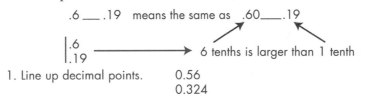

.6 ___ .19   means the same as   .60 ___ .19

| .6
| .19 ⟶ 6 tenths is larger than 1 tenth

1. Line up decimal points.   0.56
0.324

2. Look at place value: 5 tenths is larger than 3 tenths, so **0.56** is larger than **0.324**.

Converting Decimals

✪ Decimal to Fraction

To change a decimal to a fraction, use place value.

1. Decide whether the decimal represents tenths, hundredths, thousandths, etc.
2. Write the numerical part of the decimal over the appropriate power of 10—over 10 if the decimal was in the tenths place, over 100 if the decimal was in the hundredths place, and so on.

Converting Decimals, continued
✪ Decimal to Fraction, continued

3. Reduce the fraction.

Example:
.05 is 5 hundredths.

$$\frac{5}{100} \qquad \frac{5}{100} \div \frac{5}{5} = \frac{1}{20}$$

✪ Decimal to Percent
To change a decimal to a percent, move the decimal point.
1. Move the decimal point two places to the right.
2. Add a percent sign (%).
3. Add zeros for placeholders if necessary.

Examples:
.72 = 72%   .8 = 80%
.523 = 52.3%   .09 = 9%

✪ Fraction to Decimal
To find the decimal for a fraction: ⅜

1. Divide the numerator by the denominator.

$$8\overline{)3}$$

2. Add a decimal point and zeros to the dividend. Bring the decimal point straight up to the quotient.

$$8\overline{)3.00}$$

3. Divide as normal; write the answer with the decimal point.

$$\begin{array}{r} .375 \\ 8\overline{)^2 3.^100} \\ -2\ 4 \\ \hline {}^5 6^1 0 \\ -5\ 6 \\ \hline 40 \\ -40 \\ \hline 0 \end{array}$$

MATH DICTIONARY FOR KIDS

Dividing Decimals

1. Write the problem as normal.
2. Bring the decimal point straight up.
3. Divide as normal.

```
       1.57
   4 ) 6.28
      −4
      ───
       22
      −20
      ───
       28
      −28
      ───
        0
```

Multiplying Decimals

1. Write and solve the problem as normal.
2. Count the total number of places after each decimal in the numbers being multiplied.
3. Position the decimal the same number of places in the answer.

```
     3.15
   × 2.7
   ──────
     2205
  + 6300
   ──────
    8.505
```

Subtracting Decimals

1. Line up the decimal points so that the place value is in line.
2. Subtract as normal. Zeros can be added after the decimal point in order to make subtracting easier, and it won't change the answer.
3. Bring the decimal point straight down into the answer.

```
     7  2 10
   6 8. 3 0
   − 4. 69
   ────────
    63. 61
```

QUICK REFERENCE GUIDE: DIVISION

Algorithm Division

1. Write a multiples table for the divisor.
2. Start with the first digit in the dividend. Can it be divided by the divisor? If not, hold the place with a zero.
3. Look at the first two digits. Can they be divided? If so, check the multiples table to see how many times the divisor can be subtracted. Subtract it.
4. Continue in this way until you can divide no more and your remainder is smaller than the divisor.

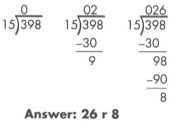

Answer: 26 r 8

Multiples Table for 15

1	15
2	30
3	45
4	60
5	75
6	90
7	105
8	120
9	135

Larger Numbers: Multiples Table

1. Make a multiples table for the number you are dividing by, the divisor.
2. Subtract the largest multiple of the divisor that does not exceed the dividend.
3. When you can't subtract any more multiples of 100s, begin subtracting multiples of 10s, and then multiples of 1 through 9.
4. When you can't subtract any more multiples, add the number of multiples that have been subtracted. This final number is the quotient.

Larger Numbers: Multiples Table, continued

Multiples Table for 53

1	53	11	583
2	106	20	1,060
3	159	30	1,590
4	212	40	2,120
5	265	50	2,650
6	318	60	3,180
7	371	70	3,710
8	424	80	4,240
9	477	90	4,770
10	530	100	5,300

```
            100 + 60 + 0
      53) 8531
          -5300
           3231
          -3180
             51
```

Answer: 160 r 51

Repeated Subtraction

15 was subtracted a total of five times with 4 remaining, so the answer is **5 r 4** or **5 ⁴⁄₁₅.**

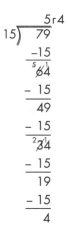

Use Manipulatives

Use beans, counters, or other objects, or draw a picture. Count out the number of beans that need to be divided. Divide them equally into the number of groups that are you are dividing by.

$61 \div 9 = 6 \text{ r } 7$

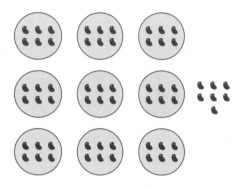

Use tiles or paper squares. Count out the number of tiles that need to be divided. Put them into the number of rows you are dividing by. Count the number of columns you are about to make, and then count the remainder.

$25 \div 4 = 6 \text{ r } 1$

QUICK REFERENCE GUIDE: FRACTIONS

Adding Fractions

To add fractions, first look at the denominators.

✪ Same Denominators

1. Leave the denominator the same, and write it in your answer.
2. Add the numerators.
3. Write the sum over the denominator.
4. Reduce (simplify) if needed.

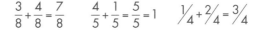

$$\frac{3}{8} + \frac{4}{8} = \frac{7}{8} \qquad \frac{4}{5} + \frac{1}{5} = \frac{5}{5} = 1 \qquad \frac{1}{4} + \frac{2}{4} = \frac{3}{4}$$

✪ Different Denominators

1. Find a common denominator.
2. Make equivalent fractions.
3. Add the numerators.
4. Write the sum over the common denominator.
5. Reduce (simplify) if needed.

$$\begin{array}{l} \frac{1}{6} \times \frac{3}{3} = \frac{3}{18} \\ + \frac{4}{18} \quad = \frac{4}{18} \\ \hline \qquad \quad \frac{7}{18} \end{array} \qquad\qquad \begin{array}{l} \frac{3}{5} \times \frac{3}{3} = \frac{9}{15} \\ + \frac{1}{3} \times \frac{5}{5} = \frac{5}{15} \\ \hline \qquad\qquad \frac{14}{15} \end{array}$$

Comparing Fractions

There are several ways to compare fractions.

✪ Find a Common Denominator

Find a common denominator for both fractions, and then compare the two fractions to determine which is larger.

Which is larger, ⁵⁄₇ or ⁹⁄₁₀?

$$\frac{5}{7} \times \frac{10}{10} = \frac{50}{70} \qquad \frac{9}{10} \times \frac{7}{7} = \frac{63}{70}$$

⁶³⁄₇₀ is larger than ⁵⁰⁄₇₀, so ⁹⁄₁₀ is larger than ⁵⁄₇.

Comparing Fractions, continued

✪ Cross Multiply

Multiply the numerator of one fraction by the denominator of the other. Repeat the process with the other two numbers, and compare the two products to determine which fraction is larger.

$$\frac{3}{4} \diagdown \frac{2}{3}$$

$3 \times 3 = 9$
$4 \times 2 = 8$
9 is greater than 8, so ¾ is greater than ⅔.

✪ Convert Fractions to Decimals

Write each fraction as a division problem, divide to find the decimals, and then compare the decimal numbers to determine which is larger.

$$\frac{5}{6} \underline{\quad\quad} \frac{1}{2}$$

```
      .83              .5
6) 4 5.¹00        2) 1.0
  -4 8             -10
    20               0
  - 18
     2
```

.83 is greater than .5,
so $\frac{5}{6}$ is greater than $\frac{1}{2}$.

Converting Fractions

✪ Fraction to Decimal

To find the decimal for a fraction, divide: ⅗

1. Divide the numerator by the denominator.

$$5\overline{)3}$$

2. Add a decimal point and zeros to the dividend. Bring the decimal point straight up to the quotient.

$$5\overline{)3.00}$$

Converting Fractions, continued
✪ Fraction to Decimal, continued

3. Divide as normal, and then write the answer with the decimal point.

$$5\overline{)3.0} \quad \begin{array}{r} .6 \\ \hline 3.0 \\ -3\,0 \\ \hline 0 \end{array}$$

✪ Improper Fraction to Mixed or Whole Number

To convert an improper fraction to a mixed or whole number, use division.

1. Divide the numerator by the denominator.
2. Write the remainder as a fraction.

$$\frac{32}{9} \rightarrow 9\overline{)32} \rightarrow 9\overline{)^2 3^1 2} \rightarrow 3\,\tfrac{5}{9}$$
$$\begin{array}{r} 3 \\ -2\ 7 \\ \hline 5 \end{array}$$

✪ Mixed Number to Improper Fraction

To convert a mixed number to an improper fraction, use multiplication.

1. Multiply the denominator by the whole number.
2. Add the numerator to the answer.
3. Put the answer over the original denominator.

$$4\frac{2}{3} \;=\; 4\frac{^+2}{_\times3} \;=\; \frac{14}{3} \quad \text{or} \quad 4\frac{2}{3} \;=\; \frac{(4\times3)+2}{3} \;=\; \frac{14}{3}$$

3 x 4 = 12
12 + 2 = 14
¹⁴⁄₁₃

3 x 4 + 2
The denominator stays the same.

Common Denominators

To find a common denominator of two or more fractions, make lists of multiples.

Example:
⅔   Multiples of 3: 3   6   **9**   12 15 **18** 21 24 **27** 30 33
⅝   Multiples of 9: **9** **18** **27** 36 45 54 63 72 81 90 99

9, 18, and 27 are multiples of 3 and 9, so **9**, **18**, and **27** are common denominators of ⅔ and ⅝.

Common Denominators, continued

Using 9 as a common denominator, multiply both the numerator and denominator of one fraction by the number needed to produce a denominator of 9. Repeat for the second fraction. The numbers by which the fractions are multiplied will usually be different for each fraction.

$$\frac{2}{3} \times \frac{3}{3} = \frac{6}{9}$$

$$\frac{5}{9} \times \frac{1}{1} = \frac{5}{9}$$

Now that the fractions have a common denominator, they can be compared, added, or subtracted easily.

Sometimes you will only need to adjust one of the fractions.

$$\frac{1}{2} \times \frac{4}{4} = \frac{4}{8}$$

The fractions now can be compared, added, or subtracted.

$$\frac{3}{8}$$

Dividing Fractions

When fractions are divided, a reciprocal and multiplication must be used. To find a fraction's reciprocal, invert the fraction by writing the numerator on the bottom and the denominator on the top. After the fraction has been inverted, multiply the two fractions together.

✪ To divide regular fractions:
1. Invert the divisor to find the reciprocal.
2. Multiply the numerators.
3. Multiply the denominators.
4. Change the answer to a mixed or whole number.
5. Reduce (simplify) the answer if necessary.

$$\frac{3}{7} \div \frac{4}{5} = \frac{3}{7} \cdot \frac{5}{4} = \frac{15}{28}$$

✪ To divide improper fractions:
1. Invert the divisor.
2. Multiply the numerators.
3. Multiply the denominators.
4. Change the answer to a mixed or whole number.

Dividing Fractions, continued

✪ To divide improper fractions, continued

5. Reduce (simplify) the answer if necessary.

$$\frac{8}{3} \div \frac{4}{2} = \frac{8}{3} \cdot \frac{2}{4} = \frac{16}{12} = 1\frac{4}{12} \div \frac{4}{4} = 1\frac{1}{3}$$

✪ To divide fractions with mixed numbers:

1. Change any mixed numbers to improper fractions.
2. Invert the divisor.
3. Multiply the numerators.
4. Multiply the denominators.
5. Change the answer to a mixed or whole number.
6. Reduce (simplify) the answer if necessary.

$$3\frac{1}{3} \div 2\frac{3}{5} = \frac{10}{3} \div \frac{13}{5} = \frac{10}{3} \cdot \frac{5}{13} = \frac{50}{39} = 1\frac{11}{39}$$

✪ To divide fractions and whole numbers:

1. Change any whole number to its fractional equivalent.
2. Invert the divisor.
3. Multiply the numerators.
4. Multiply the denominators.
5. Change the answer to a mixed or whole number.
6. Reduce (simplify) the answer if necessary.

$$5 \div \frac{2}{3} = \frac{5}{1} \div \frac{2}{3} = \frac{5}{1} \cdot \frac{3}{2} = \frac{15}{2} = 7\frac{1}{2}$$

Finding Equivalent Fractions

There are several ways to find equivalent fractions.

✪ Multiply or Divide

Multiply or divide both the numerator and the denominator by the same number.

$$\frac{2}{7} \times \frac{3}{3} = \frac{6}{21} \qquad \frac{9}{10} \times \frac{2}{2} = \frac{18}{20}$$

$$\frac{30}{36} \div \frac{6}{6} = \frac{5}{6} \qquad \frac{5}{15} \div \frac{5}{5} = \frac{1}{3}$$

Finding Equivalent Fractions, continued

✪ Use Multiples

List the multiples for the numbers in the numerator and denominator in two separate rows. The numbers in the top row become the numerators in the equivalent fractions, while the numbers in the bottom rows become the denominators.

$$\frac{4}{5} = \begin{array}{ccccccccc} 4 & 8 & 12 & 16 & 20 & 24 & 28 & 32 & 36 \\ 5 & 10 & 15 & 20 & 25 & 30 & 35 & 40 & 45 \end{array}$$

Fractions equivalent to ⅘ are: ⁸⁄₁₀, ¹²⁄₁₅, ¹⁶⁄₂₀, ²⁰⁄₂₅, ²⁴⁄₃₀, ²⁸⁄₃₅, ³²⁄₄₀, ³⁶⁄₄₅

Finding a Fraction of a Number

There are two methods for finding a fraction (part) of a number.

✪ Draw It Out

¾ of 40 = 30   Break 40 into 4 groups, then look at 3 of them.

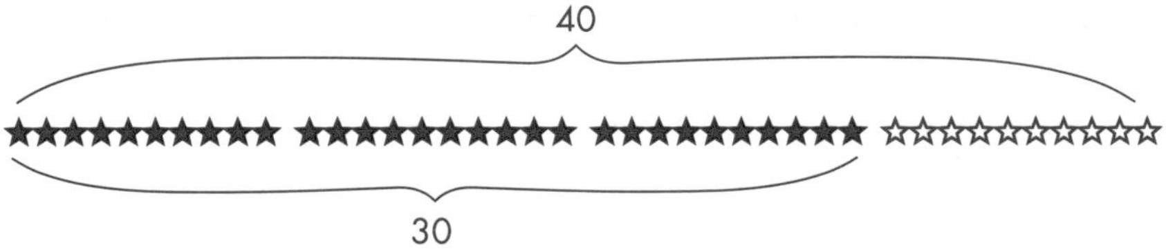

40

★★★★★★★★★★ ★★★★★★★★★★ ★★★★★★★★★★ ☆☆☆☆☆☆☆☆☆☆

30

✪ Use Division and Multiplication

1. Divide the whole number by the fraction's denominator.
2. Multiply the answer by the numerator.

Examples:
⅘ of 30

1. Divide the whole number by the denominator to find one fractional part.
   30 ÷ 5 = 6
2. Multiply the answer by the numerator of the fraction. This finds the number of fractional parts.
3. ⅘ of 30 = 24   24 is ⅘ of 30.

⁴⁄₇ of 49
- 49 ÷ 7 = 7
- 7 × 4 = 28
- 28 is ⁴⁄₇ of 49

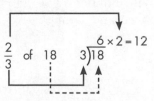

$$\frac{2}{3} \text{ of } 18 \quad 3\overline{)18} \quad 6 \times 2 = 12$$

Multiplying Fractions

The steps taken to multiply fractions depends on the type of fraction in the problem.

✪ To multiply regular fractions:

1. Multiply the numerators.
2. Multiply the denominators.
3. Reduce (simplify) the answer if necessary.

$$\frac{1}{4} \cdot \frac{3}{7} = \frac{3}{28} \qquad \frac{2}{8} \cdot \frac{4}{6} = \frac{8}{48} \div \frac{8}{8} = \frac{1}{6}$$

✪ To multiply improper fractions:

1. Multiply the numerators.
2. Multiply the denominators.
3. Change the answer to a mixed or whole number.
4. Reduce (simplify) the answer if necessary.

$$\frac{5}{3} \cdot \frac{4}{2} = \frac{20}{6} = 3\frac{2}{6} \div \frac{2}{2} = 3\frac{1}{3}$$

✪ To multiply fractions with mixed numbers:

1. Change any mixed numbers to improper fractions.
2. Multiply the numerators.
3. Multiply the denominators.
4. Change the answer to a mixed or whole number.
5. Reduce (simplify) the answer if necessary.

$$1\frac{1}{3} \cdot 2\frac{1}{5} = \frac{4}{3} \cdot \frac{11}{5} = \frac{44}{15} = 2\frac{14}{15}$$

✪ To multiply fractions with whole numbers:

1. Change any whole number to its fractional equivalent.
2. Multiply the numerators.
3. Multiply the denominators.
4. Change the answer to a mixed or whole number.
5. Reduce (simplify) the answer if necessary.

$$1\frac{1}{3} \cdot 2 = \frac{4}{3} \cdot \frac{2}{1} = \frac{8}{3} = 2\frac{2}{3}$$

Reducing Fractions

There are two common ways to reduce (simplify) a fraction to lowest terms.

✪ Use Common Factors

Find the greatest common factor of the numerator and denominator, and then divide both numbers by the factor.

$^{18}/_{27}$

1, 3, and 9 are common factors of 18 and 27. The greatest common factor is **9**, so divide the numerator and denominator by 9.

$$\frac{18}{27} \div \frac{9}{9} = \frac{2}{3}$$

$\dfrac{18}{27}$ in lowest terms is $\dfrac{2}{3}$.

✪ Use Prime Factorizations

1. Write the prime factors of each number next to the numerator and denominator.
2. Leave both of the ones alone, but cross off any other factors they have in common.
3. Multiply the numbers on each row to produce a new fraction.
4. The fraction is now in lowest terms.

$$\frac{4}{14} = \frac{1,\cancel{2},2}{1,\cancel{2},7} = \frac{1 \times 2}{1 \times 7} = \frac{2}{7}$$

Subtracting Fractions

To subtract fractions, first look at the denominators.

✪ Same Denominators

1. Leave the denominator the same, and write it in your answer.
2. Subtract the numerators.
3. Write the difference over the denominator.
4. Reduce (simplify) if needed.

$$^7/_9 - ^4/_9 = ^3/_9 \div ^3/_3 = ^1/_3 \qquad ^4/_5 - ^3/_5 = ^1/_5$$

Subtracting Fractions, continued

✪ Different Denominators

1. Find a common denominator.
2. Make equivalent fractions.
3. Subtract the numerators.
4. Write the answer over the denominator.
5. Reduce (simplify) if needed.

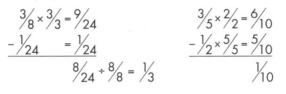

$$\frac{3}{8} \times \frac{3}{3} = \frac{9}{24}$$
$$-\frac{1}{24} \quad = \frac{1}{24}$$
$$\frac{8}{24} \div \frac{8}{8} = \frac{1}{3}$$

$$\frac{3}{5} \times \frac{2}{2} = \frac{6}{10}$$
$$-\frac{1}{2} \times \frac{5}{5} = \frac{5}{10}$$
$$\frac{1}{10}$$

QUICK REFERENCE GUIDE: MULTIPLICATION

Algorithm Multiplication

1. Start with the ones place. Multiply every number on top by that number.

$$
\begin{array}{r} 367 \\ \times\ 24 \\ \hline \end{array}
\qquad 3\ \ 2\ \ 1
\qquad
\begin{array}{l}
\text{Step 1: } 4 \times 7 = 28 \\
\text{Step 2: } 4 \times 6 = 24 \\
\text{Step 3: } 4 \times 3 = 12
\end{array}
\qquad
\begin{array}{r} {}^{2}\ {}^{2} \\ 367 \\ \times\ 24 \\ \hline 1468 \end{array}
$$

2. Once you've multiplied every digit on the top by the number in the ones place:
   - cross off any numbers you've carried so you don't get confused, and
   - circle the number in the ones place to show that you've used it, and bring that zero straight down to show that you've used it. It's going to hold your place.

$$
\begin{array}{r} {}^{2}\ {}^{2} \\ 367 \\ \times\ 24 \\ \hline 1468 \\ 0 \end{array}
$$

3. Move to the tens place. Multiply every number on the top by the digit in the tens place.

$$
\begin{array}{r} {}^{2}\ {}^{2} \\ 367 \\ \times\ 24 \\ \hline 1468 \\ 0 \end{array}
\qquad 6\ \ 5\ \ 4
\qquad
\begin{array}{l}
\text{Step 4: } 2 \times 7 = 14 \\
\text{Step 5: } 2 \times 6 = 12 \\
\text{Step 6: } 2 \times 3 = 6
\end{array}
\qquad
\begin{array}{r} {}^{1}\ {}^{1} \\ {}^{2}\ {}^{2} \\ 367 \\ \times\ 24 \\ \hline 1468 \\ 7340 \end{array}
$$

4. Add what you've recorded below to get your final answer.

$$
\begin{array}{r} {}^{1}\ {}^{1} \\ {}^{2}\ {}^{2} \\ 367 \\ \times\ 24 \\ \hline 1468 \\ +7340 \\ \hline 8808 \end{array}
$$

Break Apart

Example:
6 x 12 =
3 x 12 = 36
3 x 12 = 36

36 + 36 = 72

Break Apart
(Larger Numbers)

Example:

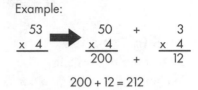

200 + 12 = 212

"Count By" Using Multiples

Example:
3 x 6 = 18
3 + 3 + 3 + 3 + 3 + 3 = 18
or 3 6 9 12 15 18

Crossed Lines
(Count Intersections)

Example:

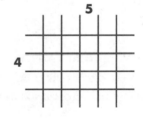

Draw a Picture

Example:
8 x 3 = 24

Window Pane Math

Example:
71 x 18 = 1,278

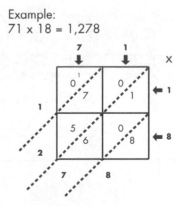

QUICK REFERENCE GUIDE: PERCENTS

Converting Percents

✪ Decimal to Percent

To change a decimal to a percent:

1. Move the decimal point two places to the right.
2. Add a percent sign (%).
3. Add zeros for placeholders if necessary.

Examples:

.35 = 35%   .293 = 29.3%
.0 = 1%   .9 = 90%

✪ Percent to a Decimal

To change a percentage to a decimal, move the decimal point two places to the left. Add zeros as placeholders if necessary.

Examples:

68% = .68   14.3% = .143
6% = .06

Finding the Percent of a Given Number

1. To find a percent, write the numbers as a fraction (part over whole).
2. Divide the numerator by the denominator.
3. Multiply the answer by 100.

I have 9 out of 18. What percent of the whole is that?

$$\frac{9}{18} = 18\overline{)9.0} \quad \rightarrow \quad .5 \times 100 = \mathbf{50\%}$$

$$\begin{array}{r} .5 \\ 18\overline{)9.0} \\ -90 \\ \hline 0 \end{array}$$

Finding the Number for a Given Percent

1. Change the percent to a decimal.
2. Multiply the decimal times the number.
3. Move the decimal point to the appropriate position in the answer.

Example:
What is 25% of 45?

```
   45
  x.25
  225        25% of 45 is 11.25.
  900
 11.25
```

QUICK REFERENCE GUIDE: PROBLEM SOLVING STEP BY STEP

When problem solving, there is often more than one way to find a correct answer. People work, think, and reason differently. A variety of strategies are shown to help you find the best strategy for the problem and for your own thinking style. The problem solving examples are some of the common methods used to solve various types of word problems. There are many more methods that can be used.

The examples shown here are analyzed by underlining with a red and blue colored pencil. The color doesn't matter, as long as two different colors are used. The purpose is to help separate and identify the question that's being asked from the information needed to solve the problem.

Acting It Out: Using a Pattern

✪ **Read the Problem**

Alexus, Paige, Alaina, and two of their friends planned on earning extra money over the summer by babysitting. They wanted to schedule fun activities for the 10 children they were watching, but there were too many children to do each activity at one time. They grouped the children into pairs and organized the activities so each group would participate at a different time without repeating any activity. Each activity would start on the hour at 1:00, 2:00, 3:00, 4:00, and 5:00. That way, each group would have completed each activity by 6:00, when they would stop for pizza. The activities chosen were swimming, biking, rock and shell hunting, canoeing, and photography. What is one way Alexus, Paige, Alaina, and their friends could organize the afternoon activities?

✪ **Analyze the Clues**

1. Use a blue colored pencil to underline the question that is being asked.
2. Use a red colored pencil to underline the information you will need to use to solve the problem.

✪ **Solve the Problem**

3. Make a chart that is six squares by six squares. The extra square on each side will allow for labelling.
4. Label the activities and the times.

	swimming	biking	rock/shell hunting	canoeing	photography
1:00					
2:00					
3:00					
4:00					
5:00					

5. Give each group of children a letter, number, symbol, or color. As there are 10 children grouped in pairs, this means there are five groups. For illustration, they are shown here as numbers 1, 2, 3, 4, and 5. Starting with the 1:00 time, place each group on the chart.

	swimming	biking	rock/shell hunting	canoeing	photography
1:00	1	2	3	4	5
2:00					
3:00					
4:00					
5:00					

6. To make sure each group continues with a different activity at a different time, move Group 1 over one space and continue numbering.

	swimming	biking	rock/shell hunting	canoeing	photography
1:00	**1**	2	3	4	5
2:00	5	**1**	2	3	4
3:00					
4:00					
5:00					

7. Continue in this manner for each time, until the chart is complete.

	swimming	biking	rock/shell hunting	canoeing	photography
1:00	**1**	2	3	4	5
2:00	5	**1**	2	3	4
3:00	4	5	**1**	2	3
4:00	3	4	5	**1**	2
5:00	2	3	4	5	**1**

QUICK REFERENCE
GUIDE: PROBLEM
SOLVING

8. An easy way to check if the work is correct is to check the diagonals. A correct chart will show the groups lined up in diagonals, as shown:

	swimming	biking	rock/shell hunting	canoeing	photography
1:00	1	2	3	4	5
2:00	5	1	2	3	4
3:00	4	5	1	2	3
4:00	3	4	5	1	2
5:00	2	3	4	5	1

❂ **Check Your Work/Record the Answer**

9. Write your answer in a complete sentence.

Because this is a diagram and can be shown, some teachers will accept "*Please see the diagram above*" as a complete sentence if the work is shown.

Alternatively, one might be expected to write the answer out: The order each group will participate in each activity is: Group 1—1:00 swimming, 2:00 biking, 3:00 rock hunting, 4:00 canoeing, 5:00 photography. Group 2—1:00 biking, 2:00 rock hunting, 3:00 canoeing, 4:00 photography, 5:00 swimming. Group 3—1:00 rock hunting, 2:00 canoeing, 3:00 photography, 4:00 swimming, 5:00 biking. Group 4—1:00 canoeing, 2:00 photography, 3:00 swimming, 4:00 biking, 5:00 rock hunting. Group 5—1:00 photography, 2:00 swimming, 3:00 biking, 4:00 rock hunting, 5:00 canoeing.

10. Explain how you know this answer is reasonable.

Each group has a different activity at a different time, and no group repeats an activity. It can easily be seen by color coding the groups that there is no color repeated in any row or column.

Drawing It Out 1: Use a Picture or Diagram to Make It Simpler

❂ **Read the Problem**

Julia grew more raspberries than she could use. She decided to share them with her family on Cloverleaf Trail near where she lived. Cloverleaf Trail faced the shore of Shamrock Lake, so the <u>houses were only on the south side of the road</u>. Julia left her house and <u>went up the road three houses to Aunt Melanie's</u>. She left there and went <u>down the road nine houses to Aunt Kathryn's</u>. Next, she walked <u>down the road three houses to Uncle Fred's</u> house, which was the <u>first house on Cloverleaf Trail</u>. <u>Uncle Billy</u> lived up the road, so Julia walked <u>up 15 houses</u> to deliver his raspberries. Julia's final stop was at <u>Aunt Mary's house four houses up</u> the road from Uncle Billy's. It was the <u>last house on Cloverleaf Trail</u>. <u>How many houses were there on Cloverleaf Trail?</u>

✪ **Analyze the Clues**

1. Use a blue colored pencil to underline the question that is being asked.

2. Use a red colored pencil to underline the information you will need to use to solve the problem.

✪ **Solve the Problem**

3. Start by looking at the basics. This problem asks for Julia to travel up or down. It could just as easily be right and left, east and west, or north and south. All that's important is that you draw a line for the road and label its end points "up" and "down." Then draw a line somewhere in the middle and label it "Julia" to represent Julia's house.

4. Next, use the clues to take the problem one step at a time, marking a place for each house, even if the clues don't say who lives at each one. Remember, Julia's starting point is her house; she's standing on that spot. You can't count the place you're at as the first step—you have to move before you can count a step. Make sure to label the houses Julia stopped at.

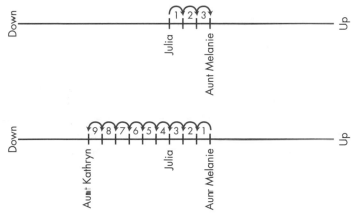

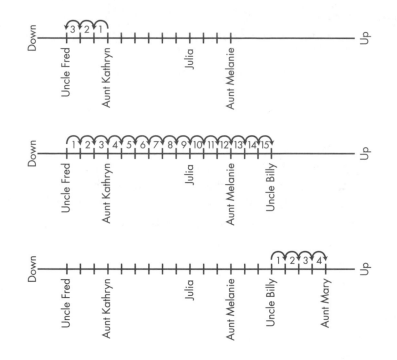

5. Now that the clues to Julia's deliveries have been drawn out and labelled, count the number of houses, represented by lines, that are on Cloverleaf Trail. Starting with Uncle Fred's house and ending with Aunt Mary's house, there are 20 altogether.

✪ Check Your Work/Record the Answer

6. Write your answer in a complete sentence.

There were 20 houses on Cloverleaf Trail.

7. Explain how you know this answer is reasonable.

When I went up the road and down the road, I made a mark for each house mentioned. For example, when Julia went up the road three houses to Aunt Melanie's, I marked 1, 2, and 3 houses, then labelled the third one Aunt Melanie. I did this each time a new clue was given. At the end I counted all of the houses, and the total was 20.

Drawing It Out 2: Identify and Use an Equation

✪ **Read the Problem**

Jimmy was trying to get to his friend's boat at the marina in Linwood. They had plans to go fishing, and Jimmy was excited to be heading out. Jimmy could take <u>Michigan Avenue, Shoreline Drive, or Bay Lane</u> to get to the Lake Huron shore. Once there, he could go through the <u>north gate, the west gate, or the service gate</u> to get to the parking lot. From the parking lot, he could get to the boat by either <u>Dock C or the Cove Walk Pathway.</u> <u>How many routes could Jimmy take to get to his friend's boat?</u>

✪ **Analyze the Clues**

1. Use a blue colored pencil to underline the question that is being asked.
2. Use a red colored pencil to underline the information you will need to use to solve the problem.

✪ **Solve the Problem**

3. This type of problem is one that can be solved with a variety of other methods, including making an organized list or drawing the problem out. However, both methods can involve doing more than what's necessary and can get confusing. To keep it simple, write an equation. First, draw out the possibilities and label them.

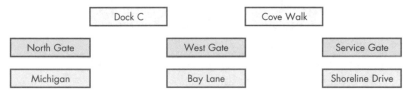

4. Now count the number of roads that could be taken. Count the gates that could be taken. Next, count the pathways to the boat.

Now write an equation. 3 roads x 3 gates x 2 paths to the dock is 3 x 3 x 2. 3 x 3 = 9, and 9 x 2 = 18.

✪ **Check Your Work/Record the Answer**

5. Write your answer in a complete sentence.

There are 18 different routes Jimmy could take to get to his friend's boat at the marina in Linwood.

6. Explain how you know this answer is reasonable.

Jimmy could take Michigan Avenue to the north gate and then to Dock C and Cove Walk Pathway. Those are two routes. He could repeat Michigan Avenue to the west gate and again to the service gate both two more times as he got to each pathway to the boat. Altogether that's a total of six routes for Michigan Avenue. If there are six for Michigan Avenue, there are also six for Bay Lane and six for Shoreline Drive. 6 + 6 + 6 = 18. Alternatively, there are three roads, three gates, and two pathways to the boat. 3 x 3 x 2 = 18 routes. Both methods give an answer of 18 routes, and the equation proves it.

Guess and Check 1: Use Parts to Find a Whole

✪ **Read the Problem**

Debbie and Kim were splitting up chores. Debbie complained that it took them <u>an hour and a half</u> to wash and dry the dishes the night before. She wasn't happy that it took her <u>three times as long to dry</u> the dishes <u>as it did for Kim to wash</u> them, so she wanted to trade. <u>How long did it take Kim to wash the dishes and Debbie to dry the dishes the night before?</u>

✪ **Analyze the Clues**

1. Use a blue colored pencil to underline the question that is being asked.
2. Use a red colored pencil to underline the information you will need to use to solve the problem.

✪ **Solve the Problem**

3. Start by setting up the times for Debbie and Kim. It took Debbie three times as long as it did Kim. That means that for every 1 minute Kim worked, Debbie had to work 3 minutes.

Kim		Debbie				
_____	+	_____	+	_____	+	_____ =

4. Next, look at the total time involved. An hour and a half was given as the total time. An hour and a half is one hour and 30 minutes.

QUICK REFERENCE GUIDE: PROBLEM SOLVING

Convert to minutes to make the problem easier to work with. Since an hour equals 60 minutes, the total time in minutes would be 90 minutes. Now you're working with the same unit of measurement.

5. Start by guessing a number. For every minute that Kim worked, Debbie worked three. Add them to find a total. Keep the goal in mind: Kim and Debbie had to use a total of 90 minutes exactly.

Kim		Debbie						
15	+	15	+	15	+	15	=	60 – too low
30	+	30	+	30	+	30	=	120 – too high
22	+	22	+	22	+	22	=	88 – too low
23	+	23	+	23	+	23	=	92 – too high
22½	+	22½	+	22½	+	22½	=	90 – exact
22½				67½				

Kim took 22½ minutes to wash dishes. Add Debbie's total to find how many minutes she worked.
22½ + 22½ + 22½ = 67½ .

✪ Check Your Work/Record the Answer

6. Write your answer in a complete sentence.

It took Kim 22½ minutes to wash dishes, and Debbie a total of 67½ minutes to dry the dishes.

7. Explain how you know this answer is reasonable.

There had to be a total of 90 minutes. Because 22 was a little too low and 23 was a little too high, the answer had to be in between the two. A guess of 22.5 (22½) proved to be correct. That gave Kim 22½ minutes to wash dishes and Debbie 67½ minutes to dry dishes. 22½ + 67½ = 90 minutes

Guess and Check 2: Write a Multiplication Equation
✪ Read the Problem

Will and Kate were selling cookies at the bake sale. Kate had taken the time to decorate her bags of chocolate cookies, so she was disappointed to find that by the end of the sale, <u>Will had sold two and a half times as many cookies as she had</u>. Will said his only secret was service with a smile. <u>Altogether, Will and Kate sold 259</u> cookies. <u>How many cookies did Will sell and how many did Kate sell?</u>

✪ Analyze the Clues

1. Use a blue colored pencil to underline the question that is being asked.
2. Use a red colored pencil to underline the information you will need to use to solve the problem.

✪ Solve the Problem

3. Write the total down to help keep it in mind. To set the problem up, remember that for every cookie Kate sold, Will sold 2½ times that. Another way to think of it is that they both sold a certain number of cookies, but then Will sold 2.5 times more.

4. Follow the steps below to use the equation to solve the problem.
   - Guess a single number of cookies they both sold.
   - Use the equation to find out how many Will sold.
   - Add Kate's total to Will's total to see if they equal 259 cookies.

   - If the total is too low or too high, try again. Persevere until you find the exact answer.

✪ Check Your Work/Record the Answer

5. Write your answer in a complete sentence.

Kate sold 74 cookies and Will sold 185 cookies.

6. Explain how you know this answer is reasonable.

Kate and Will both sold a certain number of cookies, but Will sold 2½ times more cookies. I gave them both a number of cookies and guessed at 74 cookies each. When I multiplied Will's 74 cookies by 2½, that meant Will sold 185 cookies. Kate's 74 cookies plus Will's 185 cookies equaled 259. Because they had 259 cookies to sell, and Will sold 2½ times as many as Kate, 74 and 185 had to be the number of cookies Will and Kate sold together.

Logical Reasoning 1: Balance It Out
✪ Read the Problem

Kathryn and Holly volunteered to bake several pies for the Central Elementary Field Day Picnic. They decided to make both small and large strawberry pies. They discovered when measuring that <u>two small pies and one large pie used the same amount of strawberries as seven small pies</u>. If <u>one small pie used 17 ounces</u> of strawberries, <u>how many ounces of berries did a large pie contain?</u>

✪ Analyze the Clues
1. Use a blue colored pencil to underline the question that is being asked.
2. Use a red colored pencil to underline the information you will need to use to solve the problem.

✪ Solve the Problem
3. Make a diagram that shows the equation to be balanced and label the amounts that are known.

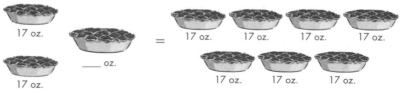

4. Cross off what each side of the equation has in common, then look at what remains to finish balancing.

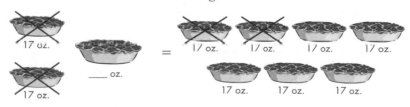

One large pie equals five small pies. There are
five small pies left, and 5 pies x 17 ounces equals
85 ounces.

$$\begin{array}{r} \overset{3}{17} \\ \underline{\times\ 5} \\ 85 \end{array}$$

✪ Check Your Work/Record the Answer

5. Write your answer in a complete sentence.

A large pie contains 85 ounces of berries.

6. Explain how you know this answer is reasonable.

Each small pie uses 17 ounces of berries. When you cross off the two pies that
each side has in common, that leaves one large pie to equal five small pies. Five
pies x 17 ounces each equals 85 ounces. That means that each large pie has to
equal 85 ounces.

Logical Reasoning 2: Use Process of Elimination With a Picture

✪ Read the Problem

Chessa, Hogan, Karli, and Samantha were at the ice cream store in Pinconning.
They had narrowed the choices to mint chocolate chip, brownie chocolate
almond, strawberry cream, and peanut butter swirl. Use the following clues to
determine which person chose each ice cream:

- Hogan and the girl who picked strawberry cream didn't like nuts.
- Chessa loves peanut butter.
- Samantha usually chose strawberry cream, but decided she wanted to try a
  new flavor this time.

✪ Analyze the Clues

1. Use a blue colored pencil to underline the question that is being
   asked.
2. Use a red colored pencil to underline the information you will need
   to use to solve the problem.

✪ Solve the Problem

3. Make a picture that shows the information known at the start of
   the problem. In this case, the people's names are known, as are the
   flavors of ice cream. Draw a picture and label it.

4. In elimination problems, it is as important to look at what's not said as what is said. At first, all that is known is that Chessa loves peanut butter. Given the clues, that means if she chose peanut butter, no one else could choose peanut butter, and she would not choose another flavor.

5. The next important clue is that Hogan and the girl who picked strawberry cream did not like nuts. That means that if the girl picked strawberry cream, Hogan did not pick that flavor. Because he also did not like nuts, Hogan would not have picked brownie chocolate almond either. That leaves Hogan with mint chocolate chip. If Hogan chose mint chocolate chip, that means that neither Karli nor Samantha could have.

6. The last clue was that Samantha normally picked strawberry cream, but this time she picked something new. If she picked something new, the only flavor left besides strawberry cream is brownie chocolate almond.

mint chocolate   brownie chocolate almond   strawberry cream   peanut butter swirl

Hogan   ~~Hogan~~ Samantha   ~~Hogan~~ ~~Samantha~~   Chessa

7. That leaves Karli with either brownie chocolate almond or strawberry cream. Because Samantha already chose brownie chocolate almond, Karli had to have strawberry cream.

mint chocolate   brownie chocolate almond   strawberry cream   peanut butter swirl

Hogan   ~~Hogan~~ Samantha   ~~Hogan~~ ~~Samantha~~ Karli   Chessa

✪ Check Your Work/Record the Answer

8. Write your answer in a complete sentence.

At the ice cream store, Chessa chose peanut butter swirl, Hogan picked mint chocolate chip, Karli had strawberry cream, and Samantha selected brownie chocolate almond.

9. Explain how you know this answer is reasonable.

Because Chessa loved peanut butter, that choice was a given. Hogan didn't like nuts and he's not a girl, so he didn't choose brownie chocolate almond or strawberry cream. He had to have mint chocolate chip. That left only brownie chocolate almond or strawberry cream for Karli and Samantha. Because Samantha didn't pick strawberry cream, she had to have brownie chocolate almond. That left strawberry cream for Karli.

Making an Organized List: Follow a Pattern

✪ **Read the Problem**

Cassie's sister challenged her to a jewelry making contest. The girls decided Cassie would make bracelets using <u>only four bead sizes: 1, 2, 3, and 4</u>. She had to <u>use each size bead in every bracelet</u>, but <u>each size could only be used once in a bracelet</u>. No <u>bracelet could be the same</u> as any other bracelet. <u>If she used all four sizes in each bracelet, how many different bracelets could Cassie make?</u>

✪ **Analyze the Clues**

1. Use a blue colored pencil to underline the question that is being asked.
2. Use a red colored pencil to underline the information you will need to use to solve the problem.

✪ **Solve the Problem**

3. Write the numbers you have to use at the top of your work. In this case those are 1, 2, 3, and 4. Colors are used below for illustration purposes.
4. Start by using 1, 2, 3, and 4 in that order.

5. To continue, keep the 1 and 2 in their position, and switch the 3 and 4.

6. You can still use the 1 in the first position, but the 2 has been used all the ways it can be used in that position with the 3 and 4. That means the 2 should be switched with the 3. Now the 2 and 4 can be used as 2, 4 and 4, 2.

7. The 3 has now been used all the ways it can be used in the second position, so it needs to be switched with the 4. Repeat as before with the 2 and 3 in the ending positions.

8. At this point, the 1 has been used as many times in that position as it can be used, and the following pattern will be present:

    1 2 3 4

    1 2 4 3

    1 3 2 4

    1 3 4 2

    1 4 2 3

    1 4 3 2

9. Continue in the same organized pattern with the 2, 3, and 4 in the first position. When complete, the organized pattern will look as follows:

1 2 3 4	2 1 3 4	3 1 2 4	4 1 2 3
1 2 4 3	2 1 4 3	3 1 4 2	4 1 3 2
1 3 2 4	2 3 1 4	3 2 1 4	4 2 1 3
1 3 4 2	2 3 4 1	3 2 4 1	4 2 3 1
1 4 2 3	2 4 1 3	3 4 1 2	4 3 1 2
1 4 3 2	2 4 3 1	3 4 2 1	4 3 2 1

10. Once this problem-solving strategy has been mastered, one can use multiplication to help solve it. For example, if you've found the first number the first position can be used a total of six times, and you have a total of four numbers to use in the first position, four numbers times six combinations equals a total of 24 combinations.

✪ **Check Your Work/Record the Answer**

   11. Write your answer in a complete sentence.

   Cassie could make 24 different bracelets.

   12. Explain how you know this answer is reasonable.

   Each number could be used a total of six times in the first position in an organized pattern. There were four numbers to use in that position. Four numbers multiplied by six ways to arrange each equals 24 different arrangements.

Modeling

Modeling is a way to make problems easier to visualize and solve by building them with Cuisenaire rods or drawing them out. Below is only one example to show how modeling can be used. There are many more. Like most things, the more one uses this type of problem solving the easier it gets to apply it to a wide variety of problems.

✪ **Read the Problem**

Fred bought a bag of his favorite fruity jellybeans to eat during the movie he planned on watching that night. Out of the bag of <u>60 beans</u>, <u>Fred ate 40%</u> of them himself, then <u>he gave ¾ of what was left to his friend</u> Diane. <u>How many jellybeans did Fred have left?</u>

✪ **Analyze the Clues**

   1. Use a blue colored pencil to underline the question that is being asked.

   2. Use a red colored pencil to underline the information you will need to use to solve the problem.

✪ **Solve the Problem**

   3. Show what you know with a model.

100%

60 jellybeans

When Fred bought the bag, the whole package had 60 beans.
In this case, 100% of the bag equals 60 beans.

Break the whole into 10 equal pieces to make it easier to work with. Because 10 sixes equal 60, you can label it. Next, look at 40% of the pieces. 10% = 6, so 6 x 4 = 24, or 40%.

					100%					
				60 jellybeans						
6	6	6	6	6	6	6	6	6	6	
10%	10%	10%	10%	10%	10%	10%	10%	10%	10%	

Fred gave ¾ of what was left to his friend, so now break what is left into four equal, or even, pieces.

					100%					
				60 jellybeans						
6	6	6	6	6	6	6	6	6	6	
10%	10%	10%	10%	10%	10%	10%	10%	10%	10%	

There were 60% of the beans left after Fred ate his. Each 10% equaled six beans, and 6 x 6 = 36 left. Break that 36 into four equal pieces. 36 ÷ 4 pieces = 9 in each piece.

					100%					
				60 jellybeans						
6	6	6	6	6	6	6	6	6	6	
10%	10%	10%	10%	10%	10%	10%	10%	10%	10%	

Fred ate | 9 | 9 | 9 | 9 |

Fred gave away   beans left

Look at 3 of those 4 pieces to find what Fred gave to Diane. Three groups of nine is 27. That left nine beans for Fred's snack later.

✪ Check Your Work/Record the Answer

4. Write your answer in a complete sentence.

Fred had nine beans left.

5. Explain how you know this answer is reasonable.

This is reasonable because 60 beans was 100% of the total. Forty percent of 60 equals 24. That left 36 beans. Thirty-six broken into fourths equals nine beans in each fourth because 36 ÷ 4 = 9. Diane got ¾ of those, and 3 x 9 = 27. That left nine beans for Fred. It can be proven with addition: 24 + 27 = 51, and 51 + 9 = 60. Sixty beans was 100% of the beans accounted for.

Using or Making a Table: Follow a Double Pattern
✪ Read the Problem

Hogan and Karli were looking for fish in the pond near Sand Lake. On the <u>first day</u>, they spotted <u>five black bass and five northern pike</u>. The <u>second day</u> they saw <u>seven black bass and 10 northern pike</u>. By the <u>third day</u>, Chessa joined in the search and they were able to spot <u>10 black bass and nine northern pike</u> swimming by. On the <u>fourth day</u>, <u>12 black bass and 14 northern pike</u> were seen. If they <u>kept seeing the fish at this same rate</u>, <u>when would Hogan, Karli, and Chessa see the same number of black bass and northern pike?</u>

✪ Analyze the Clues
1. Use a blue colored pencil to underline the question that is being asked.
2. Use a red colored pencil to underline the information you will need to use to solve the problem.

✪ Solve the Problem
3. Show what you know from the clues by drawing a chart as a place to begin. Make sure to save a space between the days and the work so you have room to write down the pattern as you work:

Days	1	2	3	4	5	6	7	8	9	10	11	12
black bass	5	7	10	12								
northern pike	5	10	9	14								

4. Determine what the pattern is for the black bass, and extend it out a bit. In this case it's +2, +3, +2, +3, and so on.

Days	1	2	3	4	5	6	7	8	9	10	11	12
		+2	+3	+2	+3	+2	+3	+2	+3			
black bass	5	7	10	12	15	17	20	22	25	27	30	32
northern pike	5	10	9	14								

5. Determine what the pattern is for the northern pike (+5, -1, +5, -1, and so on), and extend it out until you find the day that the same number of black bass and northern pike are seen in the pond.

Days	1	2	3	4	5	6	7	8	9	10	11	12
		+2	+3	+2	+3	+2	+3	+2	+3			
black bass	5	7	10	12	15	17	20	22	25	27	30	32
northern pike	5	10	9	14	13	18	17	22				
		+5	-1	+5	-1	+5	-1	+5				

6. Circle your answer.

Days	1	2	3	4	5	6	7	8	9	10	11	12
		+2	+3	+2	+3	+2	+3	+2	+3			
black bass	5	7	10	12	15	17	20	22	25	27	30	32
northern pike	5	10	9	14	13	18	17	22				
		+5	-1	+5	-1	+5	-1	+5				

✪ Check Your Work/Record the Answer

7. Write your answer in a complete sentence.

Hogan, Karli, and Chessa would have seen the same number of fish on Day 8 when they saw 22 black bass and 22 northern pike.

8. Explain how you know this answer is reasonable.

I wrote the pattern down for each fish as I solved the problem so that I could make sure the rate was accurate. The pattern for black bass was +2, +3, +2, +3. The pattern for northern pike was +5, −1, +5, −1. When both of those patterns are extended at the same rate, they end up being the same on Day 8 with 22 of each kind of fish.

Working Backwards 1: Start at the End Using a Fixed Point
✪ Read the Problem

Michelle and Elise were in charge of serving food at the concession stand at the fun fair. There were five fewer hot pretzels sold than hot dogs. There were ¼ as many hot dogs sold as cookies. There were three more cookies sold than popsicles. There were half as many popsicles sold as sodas. They sold 178 sodas. How many hot pretzels, hot dogs, cookies, popsicles, and sodas were sold, and how many items did Michelle and Elise sell altogether at the fun fair's concession stand?

✪ Analyze the Clues

1. Use a blue colored pencil to underline the question you need to answer.
2. Use a red colored pencil to underline the information you will need to use to solve the problem.

✪ Solve the Problem

3. Organize what you know by starting at the end and working your way up through the problem. Write down each item sold in order from the end.

_____ sodas

_____ ½ popsicles as sodas

_____ 3 more cookies than popsicles

_____ ¼ hot dogs as cookies

_____ 5 fewer pretzels as hot dogs

4. The first step is to write in the number of sodas sold.

<u>178</u> sodas

_____ ½ popsicles as sodas

_____ 3 more cookies than popsicles

_____ ¼ hot dogs as cookies

_____ 5 fewer pretzels as hot dogs

5. Next work the problem in order from the sodas. Pay close attention to the key words. One-half as many means ÷ 2; 3 more means + 3, ¼ as many means ÷ 4, and 5 fewer means – 5.

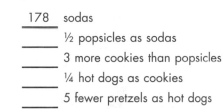

178 sodas ÷ 2 = 89 popsicles	3 more cookies than popsicles = 92 cookies	92 cookies ÷ 4 = 23 hot dogs	5 fewer pretzels than hot dogs = 18 pretzels
$\begin{array}{r} 89 \\ 2\overline{)178} \\ -16 \\ \hline 18 \\ -18 \\ \hline 0 \end{array}$	→ 89 + 3 = 92 →	$\begin{array}{r} 23 \\ 4\overline{)92} \\ -8 \\ \hline 12 \\ -12 \\ \hline 0 \end{array}$	→ 23 – 5 = 18

178	sodas
89	½ popsicles as sodas (÷ 2)
92	3 more cookies than popsicles (+ 3)
23	¼ hot dogs as cookies (÷ 4)
18	5 fewer pretzels as hot dogs (− 5)

6. To find out how much was
   sold altogether, add them up.

$$\begin{array}{r} \overset{3\,3}{178} \\ 89 \\ 92 \\ 23 \\ + 18 \\ \hline 400 \end{array}$$

QUICK REFERENCE GUIDE: PROBLEM SOLVING

✪ Check Your Work/Record the Answer

7. Write your answer in a complete sentence.

Michelle and Elise sold 178 sodas, 89 popsicles, 92 cookies, 23 hot dogs, and 18 pretzels. Altogether they sold 400 items at the fun fair concession stand.

8. Explain how you know this answer is reasonable.

Start with the 178 sodas. Half as many means that something is being divided into two pieces, and you look at one of those pieces. Since there were half as many popsicles as sodas, 178 ÷ 2 = 89 popsicles. Then, I had to add on three to the number of popsicles to equal the number of cookies, and 89 + 3 = 92. Next, when there is ¼ of something, that means it's divided into four equal pieces. Because there were ¼ as many hot dogs and cookies, I divided the number of cookies by four to find out what ¼ would be. 92 ÷ 4 = 23 hot dogs. Finally, there are five fewer pretzels than hot dogs, so I had to take the number of hot dogs and subtract five to get the number of hot pretzels. 23 − 5 = 18 hot pretzels. To find out how many sold altogether, each item had to be added together. 178 + 89 + 92 + 23 + 18 = 400.

Working Backwards 2: Start at the End Using the Remainder
✪ Read the Problem

Jack and his three friends had been counting the number of people they saw on the beach. At the end of the first hour, they'd seen half of all the people they were going to see all day. By the second hour they'd seen ¼ as many people as they did in the first hour. By the time the third hour had passed, they'd seen half the number of people they saw in the second hour. In the fourth hour they saw three times as many as they had in the third hour. At the end of the day, they saw only six people left at the beach, which was ⅔ as many as they'd seen in the fourth hour. How many people did Jack and his friends see at the beach?

⊙ **Analyze the Clues**

1. Use a blue colored pencil to underline the question that is being asked.
2. Use a red colored pencil to underline the information you will need to use to solve the problem.

⊙ **Solve the Problem**

3. Organize what you know by starting at the end and working your way up through the problem. Write down each item sold in order from the end.

_____	1st hour: ½ of all they were going to see
_____	2nd hour: ¼ as many as in 1st hour
_____	3rd hour: ½ as many as in 2nd hour
_____	4th hour: Three times as many as in 3rd hour
6	End of day: Six people left, ⅔ as many as in 4th hour

4. The only number you know for sure is that there are six people left at the beach. The rest will require perseverance and critical thinking. If there were six people left at the beach, and that was ⅔ as many as they saw in hour 4, you need to look at the fraction. Two thirds means there are three groups and you're looking at only two of them. There are six people altogether in those two groups. When you have it drawn out with all three groups, one can see that there had to be 9 people altogether in hour 4.

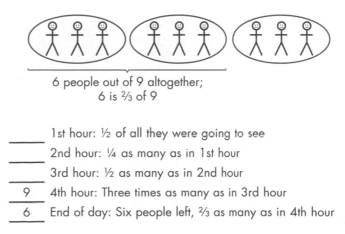

6 people out of 9 altogether;
6 is ⅔ of 9

_____	1st hour: ½ of all they were going to see
_____	2nd hour: ¼ as many as in 1st hour
_____	3rd hour: ½ as many as in 2nd hour
9	4th hour: Three times as many as in 3rd hour
6	End of day: Six people left, ⅔ as many as in 4th hour

5. In the fourth hour, there were three times as many as in hour 3. There were nine people seen in hour 4, so you need to find three times a number to equal the nine people in hour 4. 3 x 3 = 9, so there had to be three people in hour 3.

_____	1st hour: ½ of all they were going to see
_____	2nd hour: ¼ as many as in 1st hour
3	3rd hour: ½ as many as in 2nd hour
9	4th hour: Three times as many as in 3rd hour
6	End of day: Six people left, ⅔ as many as in 4th hour

6. The third hour had half as many as in hour 2. Half as many means divided by 2. If there were three people in hour 3, that means there had to be six people in hour 2. That's because 6 ÷ 2 = 3.

_____	1st hour: ½ of all they were going to see
6	2nd hour: ¼ as many as in 1st hour
3	3rd hour: ½ as many as in 2nd hour
9	4th hour: Three times as many as in 3rd hour
6	End of day: Six people left, ⅔ as many as in 4th hour

7. The second hour had 1/4 as many as in hour 1. One fourth means something is broken into four equal pieces and you're looking at only one of them. If one of those four equal pieces has six people in it, you need to look at four of those sized pieces to see how many people there were in all. Four groups of six equals 24 people altogether in the first hour.

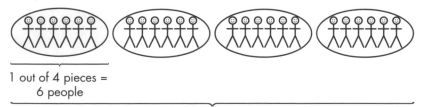

1 out of 4 pieces = 6 people

4 out of 4 pieces = 24 people

	1st hour: ½ of all they were going to see
6	2nd hour: ¼ as many as in 1st hour
3	3rd hour: ½ as many as in 2nd hour
9	4th hour: Three times as many as in 3rd hour
6	End of day: Six people left, ⅔ as many as in 4th hour

8. In order to determine how many people they saw in all, use an addition equation to add up all of the people they saw in each segment of the timeline. 24 + 6 + 3 + 9 + 6 = 48 people.

✪ Check Your Work/Record the Answer

9. Write your answer in a complete sentence.

Jack and his three friends saw 48 people at the beach.

10. Explain how you know this answer is reasonable.

The first clue gives you a means to double check the work. Because they saw half of all the people they were going to see in the first hour, I looked at the total and cut it in half. 24 is half of 48, so I know the first hour is correct. From that point, I could just use the rest of the clues to find the total number. Six is ¼ of 24, three is 1/2 of six, nine is three multiplied by three, and six is 2/3 of nine. They ended up seeing six people, and they began with 24. The clues could be followed from beginning to end, with the same numbers.

LEARNING WITH MANIPULATIVES

LEARNING WITH MANIPULATIVES: BASE 10s

Basic Fact Multiples

The rule when building multiplication problems with Base 10s, as with tiles, is that you have to build a perfect rectangle or square in order to find the answer.

1. Write the problem; build it with Base 10s.
2. Count the multiples by drawing the problem out on graph paper; write the number problem.
3. Record work on a blank 10 x 10 grid worksheet to make a multiplication chart.

Examples:
$5 \times 6 = 30$

					6
					12
					18
					24
					30

Look for patterns in multiples, and for the division/multiplication link.

Multiplying Basic Facts

This can be completed with either a Base-10 mat or with a piece of colored paper.

1. Build the problem outside of the markings on the mat (or off the edge of the colored paper).
2. Build the solution inside the mat (or on the paper).
3. Draw the problem and the solution on graph paper.
4. Write the answer on the grid in the drawing.
5. Write the problem and solution numerically.

In this example, the problem is built with Base-10 blocks on a Base-10 work mat.

Multiplying Basic Facts, continued

Example:
3 x 4 = 12

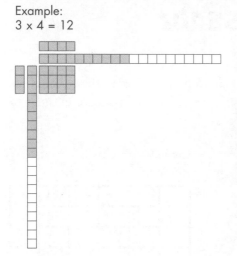

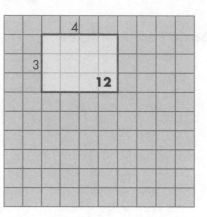

Multiplying Decimals

A Base-10 mat is made up of 100 little pieces, but is thought of as one whole piece.

1. Use unit blocks to cover the pieces, then think of money to record the answer. For example, if only 1 little square out of 100 is covered, that's like one penny, so it would be written as .01.

2. If the problem given is .4 times .6, cover 4 rows by 6 columns with unit cubes.

3. Count how many pieces are covered, and then think of money. For example, .4 x .6 has an area of .24. There are 24 units that cover it. That's like saying there are 24 out of 100 pennies, so .24 would be the answer.

Example:

Multiplying Intermediate 2-Digit x 1-Digit Problems

This can be completed with either a Base-10 mat or with a piece of colored paper.

1. Build the problem outside of the markings on the mat (or off the edge of the colored paper).
2. Build the solution inside the mat (or on the paper).
3. Draw the problem and the solution on graph paper.
4. Write the answer on the grid in the drawing.
5. Write the problem and solution numerically.
6. Use a different-colored pencil to draw the problem and the solution.

Build It

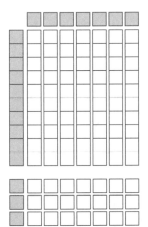

Draw It

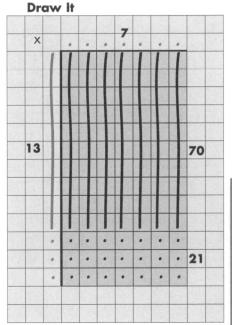

Write It

$$
\begin{array}{r}
13 \\
\times\ 7 \\
\hline
70 \\
+\ 21 \\
\hline
91
\end{array}
$$

Multiplying Intermediate 2-Digit x 2-Digit Problems

This can be done with either a Base-10 mat or with a piece of colored paper.

1. Build the problem outside of the markings on the mat (or off the edge of the colored paper).
2. Build the solution inside the mat (or on the paper).
3. Draw the problem and the solution on graph paper.
4. Write the answer on the grid in the drawing.
5. Write the problem and solution numerically.
6. Use a different-colored pencil to draw the problem and the solution.

Build It

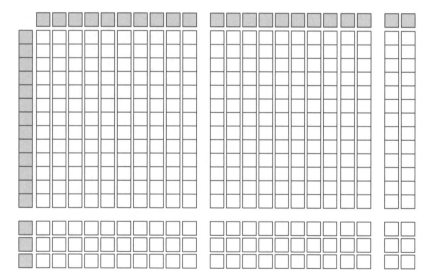

Multiplying Intermediate 2-Digit x 2-Digit Problems, continued

Draw It

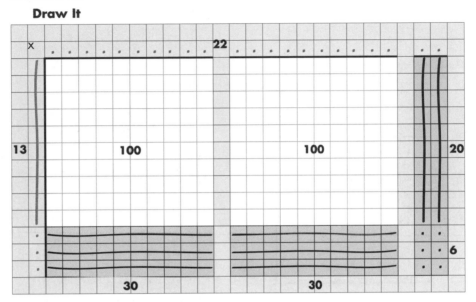

Write It

$$
\begin{array}{r}
13 \\
\times\ 21 \\
\hline
200 \\
80 \\
+\ \ \ 6 \\
\hline
286
\end{array}
$$

LEARNING WITH MANIPULATIVES: GEOBOARDS

Angles and Triangles

Geoboards can be used to model the following:

* acute, obtuse, right, and straight angles;

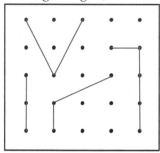

* isosceles right triangles, isosceles acute triangles, and isosceles obtuse triangles; and

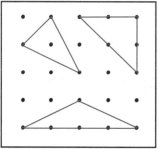

* equilateral, isosceles, and scalene triangles;

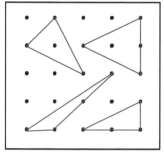

* scalene right triangles, scalene acute triangles, and scalene obtuse triangles.

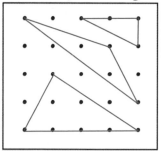

Angle Measurement

Many geoboards have the circumference of a circle outlined in pegs on the back of the board. Because every circle can be divided evenly into 360° degrees, geoboards can be used to find the measure of central angles.

To do this, use a calculator and this equation: 360 ÷ the number of same-sized angles built in the circle = the number of degrees in each angle.

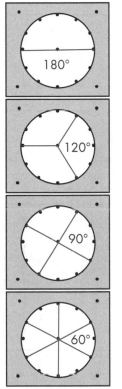

360° divided into two even pieces:
360° ÷ 2 = 180°

360° divided into three even pieces:
360° ÷ 3 = 120°

360° divided into four even pieces:
360° ÷ 4 = 90°

360° divided into six even pieces:
360° ÷ 6 = 60°

360° ÷ 12 = 30°
(not pictured)

Area: Irregular Polygons

Area of irregular polygons can be determined by breaking the shape into bits according how they make up a larger rectangle.

1. Build and draw the shape on dot paper.
2. Count whole squares first.
3. Then count halves.
4. Next, look at the remainder as part of a larger rectangle.
5. Label them on dot paper.
6. Add up the total.

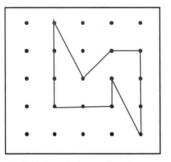

1. Build and draw the shape.

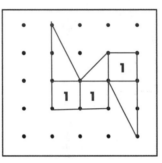

2. Count the whole squares.

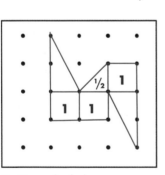

3. Count the halves.

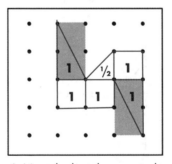

4. Next, look at the remainder as part of the rectangles they make up.

Example:
Two whole squares make up this rectangle, and half of that is used. This portion equals 1.

Area: Regular Polygons

Area of regular polygons can be determined by using the square units on the geoboard.

1. Identify the unit of measure.
2. Count the number of square units inside.
3. Don't forget to count halves.

A = 3

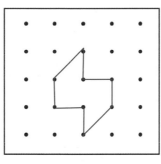
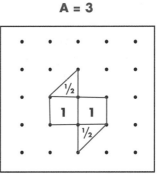

Building Polygons and Other Figures

Geoboards are useful tools to show geometric concepts. They come in a variety of pin sizes, from 5 x 5 to 11 x 11. Among other concepts, they are well suited to modeling and practicing with:

★ regular and irregular polygons;
★ angles;
★ triangles;
★ circumference, diameter, radius, and chords;
★ parallel, perpendicular, and intersecting lines; and
★ central angles and inscribed angles.

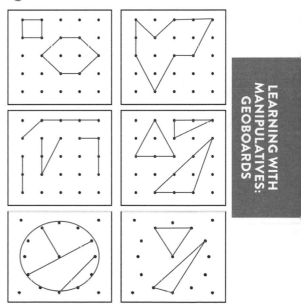

Circumference, Diameter, Radius, and Chord

Geoboards can be used to model the different parts of a circle.

★ **Circumference:** the distance around the circle.

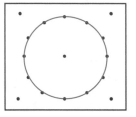

★ **Radius:** the distance from the center of the circle to a point on the circle.

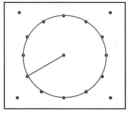

★ **Diameter:** a chord that passes through the center of the circle.

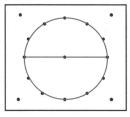

★ **Chord:** a line segment that connects two points on a circle.

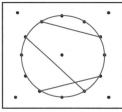

Fractions

Geoboards can be used to model fractions in several different ways.

1. Build the model; draw it on dot paper. Determine the fractional part by counting units.
2. Start with a model; draw it on dot paper. Divide it into an equal number of sections, according to the denominator.
3. Find as many ways as possible to build a certain fraction. Use a variety; for example, build ⅓, then ⅚, then ⅖.

Example 1:

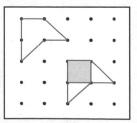

Example 2:

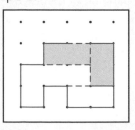

Fractions, continued

Example 3:

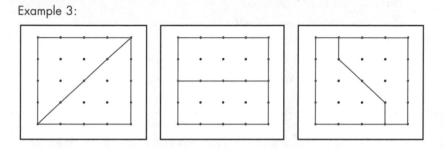

Many geoboards have the circumference of a circle outlined in pegs on the back of the board. These generally have 12 pegs, so the circle can be evenly divided into equal pieces. Each piece equals $\frac{1}{12}$, so that's the basis for conversion.

1. Write the problem on dot paper and label the fractional parts.
2. Make any necessary conversions.
3. Solve.
4. Reduce to lowest terms.

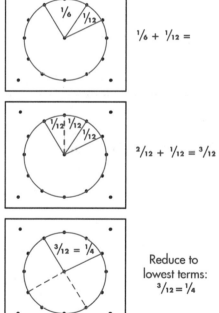

$\frac{1}{6} + \frac{1}{12} =$

$\frac{2}{12} + \frac{1}{12} = \frac{3}{12}$

Reduce to lowest terms: $\frac{3}{12} = \frac{1}{4}$

Fraction Equivalence

1. Build a model of one whole.
2. Find one way to evenly divide it.
3. Name the fractional piece.
4. Build the model again.
5. Find another way to divide it.
6. Rename it.

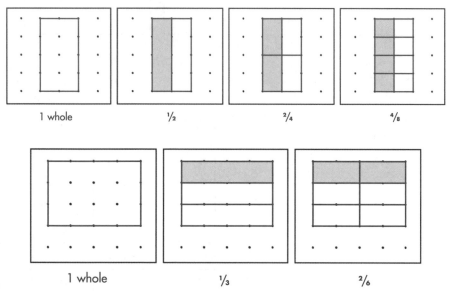

Multiplying Fractions

Geoboards can be used as a beginning step for multiplying simple fractions.

1. Use the denominators to determine the size of the rectangle that must be built. For ¾ x ½, a rectangle with an area of 4 x 2 must be drawn.
2. Next, use the numerators to decide how much of the rectangle to look at and then shade that part. In the example, look at 3 rows by 1 column.
3. Count the shaded part to find the numerator, and then count the whole rectangle to find the denominator.
4. Write the fraction as shaded part to whole part: ⅜.

Multiplying Fractions, continued

$$^3/_4 \times {}^1/_2 = {}^3/_8$$

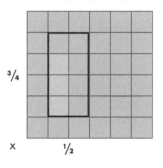

$^3/_4$

$\times$ $^1/_2$

Parallel, Perpendicular, and Intersecting Lines

Geoboards can be used to model different lines.

★ Parallel lines are in the same plane and never meet. They are the same distance apart.

★ Intersecting lines are lines that meet or cross at a point.

★ Perpendicular lines are special kinds of intersecting lines that intersect at right angles.

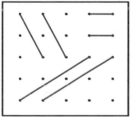

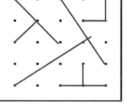

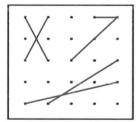

Parallel Lines   Perpendicular Lines   Intersecting Lines

LEARNING WITH MANIPULATIVES: GEOMETRIC SOLIDS

Building Models With Candy or Clay

This can be done with soft candies, gumdrops, or clay and some toothpicks. For larger solid models, toothpicks may need to be broken in half in order to sustain the shape.

1. Build the geometric shapes and solids: triangle, square, pentagon, hexagon, cube, triangular prism, rectangular prism, triangular pyramid, rectangular pyramid, pentagonal prism, and hexagonal prism.
2. Count the faces, edges, and vertices.
3. Extend by predicting how a film of bubble solution will cover the shape when dipped.
4. Submerge in bubble solution and check predictions.
5. If clay is used, it needs to be dense, solid clay to withstand repeated dunking.

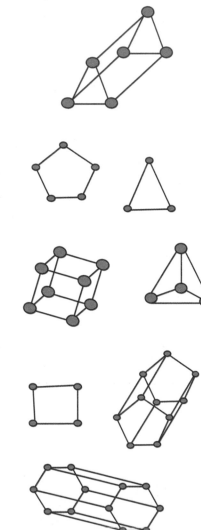

Comparing Properties

1. Make a chart or a map with one side labeled "similarities" and the other side labeled "differences."
2. Using two different geometric solids, compare and contrast the properties of the shapes.
3. Important vocabulary terms to remember when comparing and contrasting the properties include: parallel, perpendicular, faces, edges, vertices, prism, cubic, and so forth.

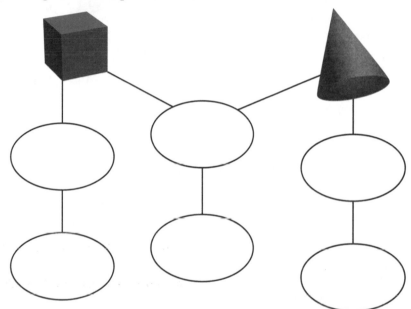

LEARNING WITH MANIPULATIVES: GRAPH PAPER

Dividing With Intersections

Drawing crossed lines can help find the answer to simple division problems. Graph paper helps to keep the problem neat and is easier to read and solve.

1. For $43 \div 6$, draw 6 lines to represent 6 rows.
2. Count the number of intersections made as intersection lines are drawn to represent columns.
3. Count as close to the number as possible without going over.
4. When as many lines as possible are drawn without going over, count the number of columns drawn.
5. Count what is left over as the remainder.
6. $43 \div 6$ has 7 columns; so the answer is 7 with a remainder of 1.

The one that is remaining

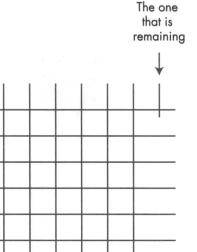

6 12 18 24 30 36 42

$43 \div 6 = 7$ columns with 1 remaining

Drawing Multiplication or Division

1. Use counters to build the problem.
2. Draw the picture out, and then write it in numbers.

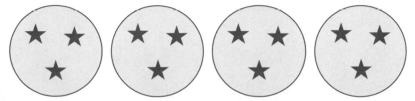

Multiplying Fractions

Graph paper can be used as an intermediate step for multiplying fractions.

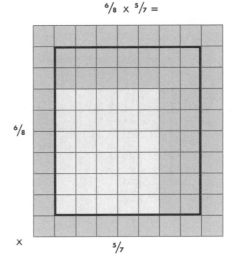

1. Use the denominators to determine the size of the rectangle that must be drawn. For $^6/_8$ x $^5/_7$, a rectangle with an area of 8 x 7 must be drawn.
2. Next, use the numerators to decide how much of the rectangle to look at and then shade that part. In the example, look at 6 rows by 5 columns.
3. Count the shaded part to find the numerator, and then count the whole rectangle to find the denominator.
4. Write the fraction as shaded part to whole part: $^{30}/_{56}$.

Multiplying Intermediate 2-Digit x 1-Digit Problems

1. Draw the problem on graph paper.
2. Draw in the solution.
3. Write the answer on the grid in the drawing.
4. Write the problem and solution numerically.
5. Use a different-colored pencil to draw the problem and the solution.

Multiplying Intermediate 2-Digit x 1-Digit Problems, continued

Draw It

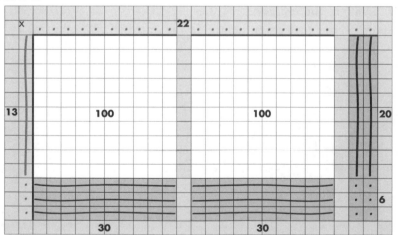

Write It

$$
\begin{array}{r}
13 \\
\times\ 7 \\
\hline
70 \\
+\ 21 \\
\hline
91
\end{array}
$$

Multiplying Intermediate 2-Digit x 2-Digit Problems

1. Draw the problem on graph paper.
2. Draw in the solution.
3. Write the answer on the grid in the drawing.
4. Write the problem and solution numerically.
5. Use a different-colored pencil to draw the problem and the solution.

Draw It

Multiplying Intermediate 2-Digit x 2-Digit Problems, continued

Write It

```
     13
   x 21
   ----
    200
     80
   +  6
   ----
    286
```

Multiplying With Window Pane Math

1. Write the problem around the outer edge of the window. Complete the simple multiplication problems and record them in the windows as shown.
2. Draw a light line through the problem when done so it isn't added by accident in the last step.
3. Finally, add the numbers within each ray, starting at the right, or the ones place, as would be done in a regular problem.

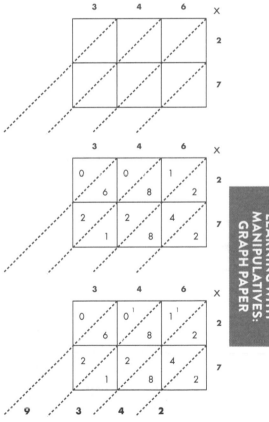

346 x 27 = 9,342

LEARNING WITH MANIPULATIVES: HUNDREDS CHARTS

Counting Multiples

Count multiples on a hundreds chart by using bingo chips or transparent game markers.

1. As each multiple of a certain number is counted orally, place a chip over the number.
2. Look for the patterns created.
3. Record the patterns on a sheet of paper.

1	2	3	4	5	6	7	8	9	10
11	12	13	14	15	16	17	18	19	20
21	22	23	24	25	26	27	28	29	30
31	32	33	34	35	36	37	38	39	40
41	42	43	44	45	46	47	48	49	50
51	52	53	54	55	56	57	58	59	60
61	62	63	64	65	66	67	68	69	70
71	72	73	74	75	76	77	78	79	80
81	82	83	84	85	86	87	88	89	90
91	92	93	94	95	96	97	98	99	100

Finding Common Multiples

1. Count multiples on a hundreds chart by using different-colored bingo chips or transparent game markers.
2. As each multiple of a certain number is counted, place a chip over the number.
3. Look for the patterns created; find the common multiples. The common multiples of two numbers are those that share two chips of different colors.
4. Record the patterns on a sheet of paper.

1	2	3	4	5	6	7	8	9	10
11	12	13	14	15	16	17	18	19	20
21	22	23	24	25	26	27	28	29	30
31	32	33	34	35	36	37	38	39	40
41	42	43	44	45	46	47	48	49	50
51	52	53	54	55	56	57	58	59	60
61	62	63	64	65	66	67	68	69	70
71	72	73	74	75	76	77	78	79	80
81	82	83	84	85	86	87	88	89	90
91	92	93	94	95	96	97	98	99	100

LEARNING WITH MANIPULATIVES: MIRRORS

Angles With Mirrors

Angles less than 180° can be measured with a hinged mirror and small object.

1. Align the mirror along an angle drawn on paper starting at the vertex.
2. Center the object in between the sides of the mirrors.
3. Count the total number of objects seen: the object on the table and those seen in the mirrors.
4. Use a calculator to divide and find the size of the angle.

Three objects total are seen, so 360 ÷ 3 = 120°.

Five objects total are seen, so 360 ÷ 5 = 72°.

Note: The drawback of this method is that it's not a precise measurement.

Line Symmetry

If a figure can be reflected, flipped, or folded over a line and it appears unchanged, that figure is said to have line symmetry. Also called reflection or fold symmetry. When folded, flipped or reflected, both sides are exactly aligned. Use a mirror to test for line symmetry.

LEARNING WITH MANIPULATIVES: PATTERN BLOCKS

Angles

Use the standard pattern blocks to measure basic, common angles.
Below is a list of the pattern block angle measurements:

★ Orange Square = 90°

★ Yellow Hexagon = 120°

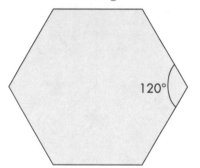

★ Small Tan Rhombus = 30°
★ Large Tan Rhombus = 150°

★ Small Blue Rhombus = 60°
★ Large Blue Rhombus = 120°

★ Small Red Trapezoid = 60°
★ Large Red Trapezoid = 120°

★ Green Triangle = 60°

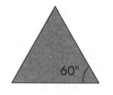

Angles With Mirrors

Use hinged mirrors to determine the angles. Angle measurement is measurement from point to point on the circumference of a circle, using the center point (hinge) as the vertex.

1. Align pattern blocks along the mirror at the vertex.
2. Look into the mirror at table-top level; count the block on the table and those that can be seen in the mirror. For example, using the orange square, a total of four squares can be seen.
3. Use a calculator to determine the angle: $360 \div 4 = 90°$ angle.

Mirror hinge at vertex: When opened up, the ends of the mirror will show the shape of a circle.

When a square is placed at the vertex, a top view will show that it's a square corner (90°) angle. Four squares total will be seen in the mirror and on the table, so $360 \div 4 = 90°$.

In this example, three rhombuses total will be seen, so $360 \div 3 = 120°$.

In this example, 12 rhombuses total will be seen, so $360 \div 12 = 30°$.

Area

Area measurement is based on same-sized pieces, or units. For example, when measuring in green triangles, all shapes in a puzzle need to be converted, or measured, in green triangles. It is important to build the model and then trace it, inside and out. Avoid using the orange and tan blocks as they don't naturally cover the other shapes.

Area, continued

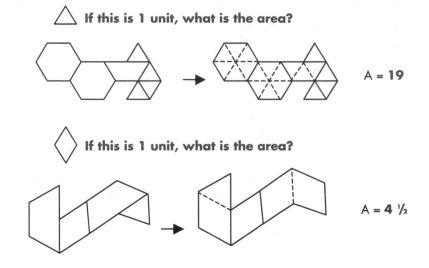

If this is 1 unit, what is the area?

A = 19

If this is 1 unit, what is the area?

A = 4 ½

Build a shape with an area of 16 (many possible answers).

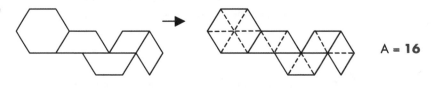

A = 16

Fractions

✪ Adding Fractions

1. Build a shape.
2. Cover it with different pieces.
3. Name those pieces by fractional size.
4. Convert those pieces to the same size.
5. Solve.

In the next example, there is more than one way to solve the problem. It can either be converted to twelfths, or it can be converted to sixths.

Fractions, continued
✪ Adding Fractions, continued

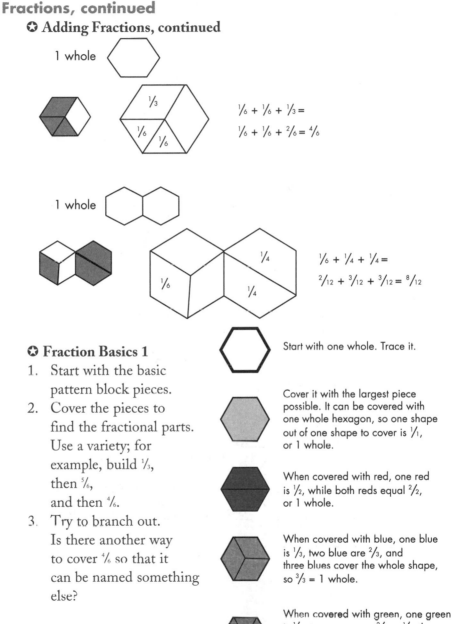

1 whole

$$\tfrac{1}{6} + \tfrac{1}{6} + \tfrac{1}{3} =$$
$$\tfrac{1}{6} + \tfrac{1}{6} + \tfrac{2}{6} = \tfrac{4}{6}$$

1 whole

$$\tfrac{1}{6} + \tfrac{1}{4} + \tfrac{1}{4} =$$
$$\tfrac{2}{12} + \tfrac{3}{12} + \tfrac{3}{12} = \tfrac{8}{12}$$

✪ Fraction Basics 1

1. Start with the basic pattern block pieces.
2. Cover the pieces to find the fractional parts. Use a variety; for example, build ⅓, then ⅚, and then ⁴⁄₆.
3. Try to branch out. Is there another way to cover ⁴⁄₆ so that it can be named something else?

Start with one whole. Trace it.

Cover it with the largest piece possible. It can be covered with one whole hexagon, so one shape out of one shape to cover is ¹⁄₁, or 1 whole.

When covered with red, one red is ½, while both reds equal ²⁄₂, or 1 whole.

When covered with blue, one blue is ⅓, two blue are ⅔, and three blues cover the whole shape, so ³⁄₃ = 1 whole.

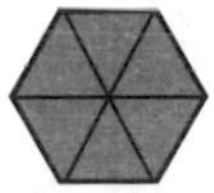

When covered with green, one green is ⅙, two green are ²⁄₆ or ⅓, three green are ³⁄₆ or ½, four green are ⁴⁄₆ or ⅔, five green are ⅚, and six green cover the whole thing, so ⁶⁄₆ = 1 whole.

Fractions, continued

✪ Fraction Basics 2

1. Start with the basic pattern block pieces.
2. Cover the pieces to find the fractional parts.
3. Trace and count to solve.
4. Fractions must be solved with same-sized pieces; generally, the smallest size works well.
5. Try to branch out. Is there another way to cover and name the shape?

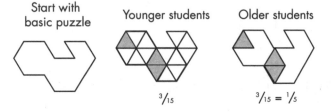

Start with basic puzzle   Younger students   Older students

$^3/_{15}$ $^3/_{15} = ^1/_5$

If the trapezoid block is ½, what is the following?

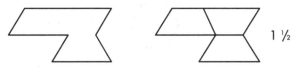

1 ½

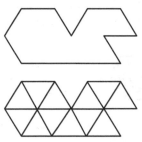

If this is one unit, what is
- one green triangle? ($^1/_{12}$)
- one blue rhombus? ($^2/_{12}$, $^1/_6$)
- one red trapezoid? ($^3/_{12}$, or $^1/_4$)
- one yellow hexagon? ($^6/_{12}$, $^3/_6$, $^2/_4$, or ½)

Fractions, continued

✪ Fraction Equivalence

1. Build a shape.
2. Cover it with pieces of one color.
3. Name it.
4. Cover it with pieces of another color.
5. Rename it.

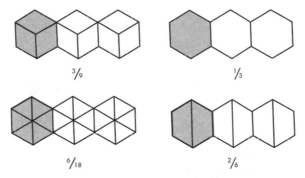

✪ Subtracting Fractions 1

★ Build a whole.
★ Cover it with the size pieces named in the problem.
★ Name those pieces by fractional size.
★ Convert those pieces to the same size.
★ Solve.

Build each part of the problem on the whole.

1 whole

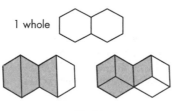

$^3/_4 - ^2/_3 =$

Cover with green triangles. Count how many green triangles were left uncovered out of how many it would have taken to cover the whole. In this case, that would be 1 uncovered out of the 12 it would take to make a whole, so $^1/_{12}$.

$^3/_4 - ^2/_3 =$

$^9/_{12} - ^8/_{12} = ^1/_{12}$

Fractions, continued

✪ Subtracting Fractions 2

1. Assign each piece a value.
2. Build the problem.
3. Cover it with the size pieces named in the problem.
4. Name those pieces by fractional size.
5. Convert those pieces to the same size.
6. Solve.

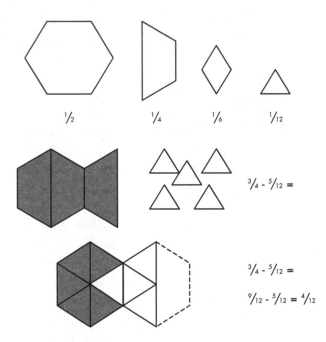

$\frac{1}{2}$ $\frac{1}{4}$ $\frac{1}{6}$ $\frac{1}{12}$

$\frac{3}{4} - \frac{5}{12} =$

$\frac{3}{4} - \frac{5}{12} =$

$\frac{9}{12} - \frac{5}{12} = \frac{4}{12}$

Build the whole and find how many green triangles it would take to cover it. That's the denominator. Then, build each part of the problem. Cover the portion being subtracted with green triangles. Count how many green triangles it would take to cover the rest. In this case, that would be 4 left out of the 12 it would take to make a whole, so $\frac{4}{12}$.

Line Symmetry

If a figure can be reflected, flipped, or folded over a line and it appears unchanged, that figure is said to have line symmetry. Also called reflection or fold symmetry. When folded, flipped, or reflected, both sides are exactly aligned. Build a figure with a line of symmetry using pattern blocks, and then use a mirror to check your work.

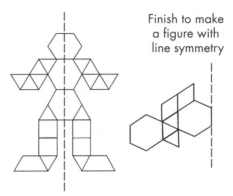

Finish to make a figure with line symmetry

Perimeter

Perimeter measurement is based on same-sized pieces, or units. In measuring perimeter with pattern blocks, the standard is the size of one side of a green triangle. The long red side equals two (2) green triangles.

The long red side has a length of two green triangles.

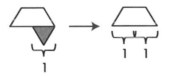

Find the perimeter.

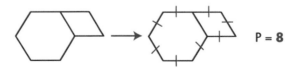

P = 8

Use two blocks to build a shape with a perimeter of 9.

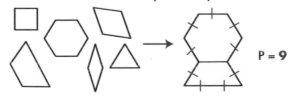

P = 9

Rotational Symmetry

Rotational symmetry is the number of ways a shape can be turned, or rotated, to fit on itself and still look the same. If it only fits on itself one time (a turn of 360°), it does not have rotational symmetry.

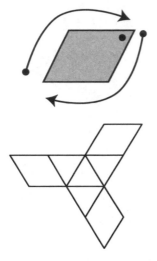

This will rotate to fit on itself two times.
That gives it a rotational symmetry of order 2.

This will rotate to fit on itself three times.
That gives it a rotational symmetry of order 3.

LEARNING WITH MANIPULATIVES: PROTRACTORS

Angle Measurement

A regular protractor has the shape of a half of a circle. A half a circle equals 180°, so a whole circle equals 360°. Two protractors together show a whole circle, or 360°. One is used for measuring angles less than 180°. Protractors are used to measure angles more precisely.

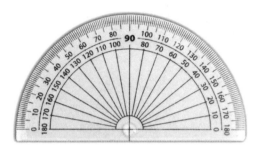

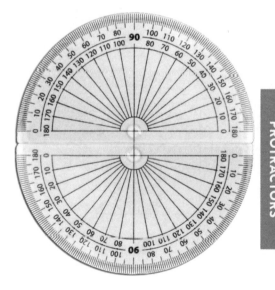

LEARNING WITH MANIPULATIVES: TANGRAMS

Angle Identification

Tangram pieces are relational, so knowing the 90° angle can help you figure out the others. Below are the angle measurements for each piece.

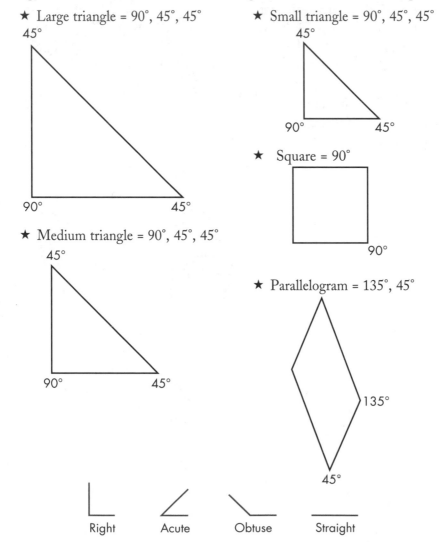

★ Large triangle = 90°, 45°, 45°

★ Small triangle = 90°, 45°, 45°

★ Square = 90°

★ Medium triangle = 90°, 45°, 45°

★ Parallelogram = 135°, 45°

Right Acute Obtuse Straight

Congruence

Congruent polygons have the same shape and the same size. The symbol for congruence is ≅.

Find two congruent triangles:

Build two congruent triangles using the following:

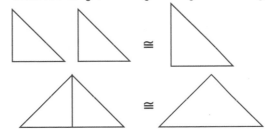

Creating Polygons

Use a specific number of tangram pieces to create given polygons. Some possibilities include:

- ★ triangles,
- ★ parallelograms,
- ★ rhomboids,
- ★ rectangles,
- ★ squares,

- ★ isosceles trapezoids,
- ★ non-isosceles trapezoids,
- ★ pentagons,

- ★ hexagons,
- ★ heptagons,
- ★ octagons,
- ★ nonagons, and
- ★ decagons.

Use five tangram pieces to make a parallelogram.

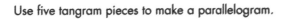

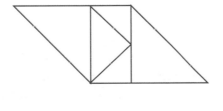

Use four tangram pieces to make an isosceles trapezoid.

Fractions

✪ Adding Fractions

1. Build shapes with tangrams.
2. Label the value of each piece. All pieces are based on the size of the small triangle, which is $\frac{1}{16}$ of the whole.
3. Add, using the basis of $\frac{1}{16}$ for conversion.

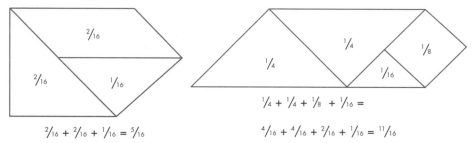

$\frac{2}{16} + \frac{2}{16} + \frac{1}{16} = \frac{5}{16}$

$\frac{1}{4} + \frac{1}{4} + \frac{1}{8} + \frac{1}{16} =$

$\frac{4}{16} + \frac{4}{16} + \frac{2}{16} + \frac{1}{16} = \frac{11}{16}$

✪ Fraction Basics 1

1. Use tangrams to find the fractional pieces of a whole. All pieces are based on the size of the small triangle, which is $\frac{1}{16}$ of the whole.
2. Determine how many small triangles it would take to make the whole square. How many large triangles would it take? How many medium triangles? How many squares?

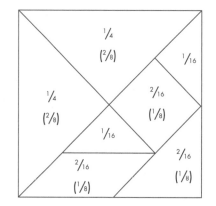

✪ Fraction Basics 2

1. Use tangrams to find the fractional pieces of a whole. All pieces are based on the size of the small triangle, which is $\frac{1}{16}$ of the whole.
2. Determine how many small triangles it would take to make various fractional parts.

Fractions, continued

✪ Fraction Basics 2, continued

If a large triangle has a value of one whole, use four pieces to find a figure with a value of 2.

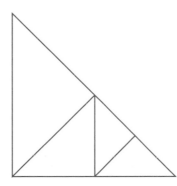

If a large triangle has a value of one whole, use three pieces to find a figure with a value of 1 ½.

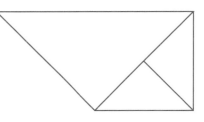

Line Symmetry

If a figure can be reflected, flipped, or folded over a line and it appears unchanged, that figure is said to have line symmetry. Also called reflection or fold symmetry. When folded, flipped or reflected, both sides are exactly aligned.

1. Build a figure with a line of symmetry using tangrams.
2. Use a mirror to check your work.

Add pieces to make a figure with line symmetry.

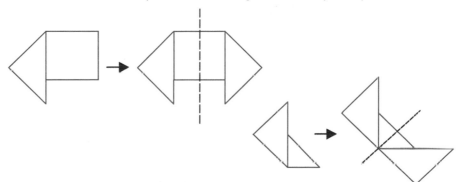

Rotational Symmetry

Rotational symmetry is the number of ways a shape can be turned, or rotated, to fit on itself and still look the same. If it only fits on itself one time (a turn of 360°), it does not have rotational symmetry.

Add more tangrams to make a polygon with rotational symmetry.

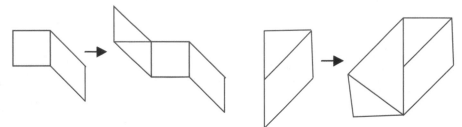

Similarity

Similar polygons have the same shape but not the same size. The symbol for similarity is ~.

Find two similar triangles:

Build two similar triangles using the following:

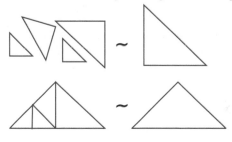

LEARNING WITH MANIPULATIVES: TILES

Basic Multiplication Facts With a Class Tile Chart

This example uses the multiplication facts for the number 3.

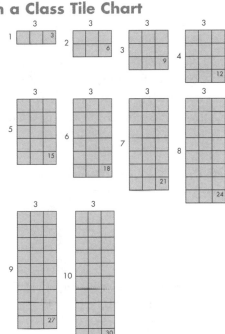

1. Use the factors 1 and 3 to build a figure with an area of 3. The figure has to be a perfect rectangle or square to be accepted.
2. Cut one out and post it on the class chart.
3. Write the factors on each side and record the total area in the bottom right corner of the shape.
4. Continue with the factors 2 and 3, then 3 and 3, and so on, until the basic facts of 3 are complete through 3 x 10.

Dividing Smaller Number Problems

1. In division, start with the total number.
2. Count out the total and put them into as many rows and columns as possible.
3. If there are leftovers, set them to the side.

Dividing Smaller Number Problems, continued

In the example shown, start by making four rows because that's the divisor. Arrange all of the tiles into those rows, until no more full rows can be made. For 22 ÷ 4, five columns can be made. When four rows of five columns are built, a total of 20 tiles are used. Subtract them from the problem. There are two tiles left, which is the remainder.

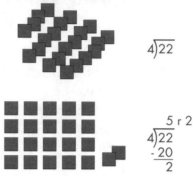

$$4\overline{)22}$$

$$\begin{array}{r} 5\ r\ 2 \\ 4\overline{)22} \\ -20 \\ \hline 2 \end{array}$$

Doubling in Multiplication

1. Build a number. The example is shown with the number 3.
2. Double one row of 3 to get two rows of 3; that makes 6.
3. Double two rows of 3 to get four rows of 3; that's 12.
4. Double four rows of 3 to get eight rows of 3; that's 24.
5. Practice doubling with all basic facts.

Multiplying Basic Facts With a 10 x 10 Grid and Tiles

1. Number the outside edges of a blank 10 x 10 grid from 1–10 along the top and the left edge.
2. Build a multiplication problem using a tile array.
3. Use two paper strips to block off the same number and shape on the 10 x 10 grid as was used in the tiles.
4. Count the tiles; record the answer in the appropriate box in the 10 x 10 grid.

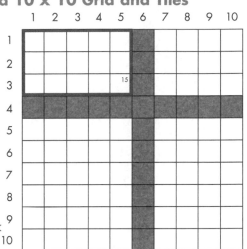

Multiplying Fractions

The denominator tells how many rows and columns to build. The numerator tells how much of the whole is being looked at.

1. Using the example of ⅔ x ⁴⁄₆, build a rectangle 3 rows by 6 columns, because that's what the denominators show.
2. Look at the part of each the numerator shows; in this case 2 rows by 4 columns. This is the shaded area.
3. Write as the part to the whole (i.e., ⁸⁄₁₈, or 8 out of 18 are shaded).

To multiply ⅔ x ⁴⁄₆:
• build a rectangle 3 rows by 6 rows, and
• then look at the area of 2 by 4.

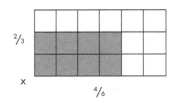

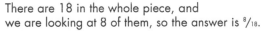

There are 18 in the whole piece, and we are looking at 8 of them, so the answer is ⁸⁄₁₈.

FORMULAS

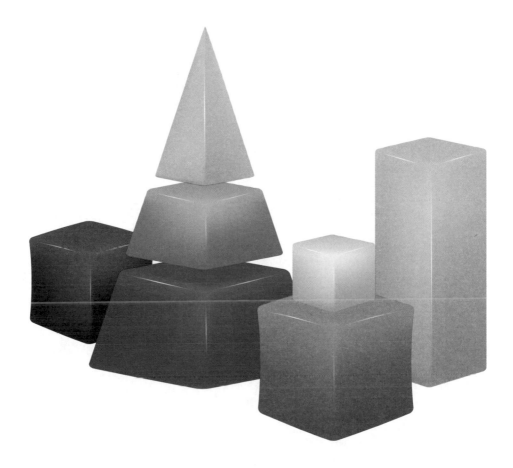

FORMULAS

Area

circle	$A = \pi r^2$	**r** is the radius
parallelogram	$A = b \times h$	**b** is the base, **h** is the height
rectangle	$A = l \times w$	**l** is the length, **w** is the width
square	$A = s^2$	**s** is the length of one side
trapezoid	$A = \frac{1}{2}h(b_1 + b_2)$	**b₁** and **b₂** are the opposite, parallel sides
triangle	$A = \frac{1}{2}(b \times h)$	**b** is the base, **h** is the height

Perimeter

circle	$C = 2\pi r$	**r** is the radius
	$C = \pi d$	**d** is the diameter
rectangle	$p = 2l + 2w$	**l** is the length, **w** is the width
square	$p = 4s$	**s** is the length of one side

Volume

cone	$V = \frac{1}{3}\pi r^2 h$	**r** is the radius, **h** is the height
cube	$V = s^3$	**s** is the length of one edge
cylinder	$V - \pi r^2 h$	**r** is the radius, **h** is the height
rectangular prism	$V = l \times w \times h$	**l** is the length, **w** is the width, **h** is the height
sphere	$V = \frac{4}{3}\pi r^3$	**r** is the radius

TABLES AND CHARTS

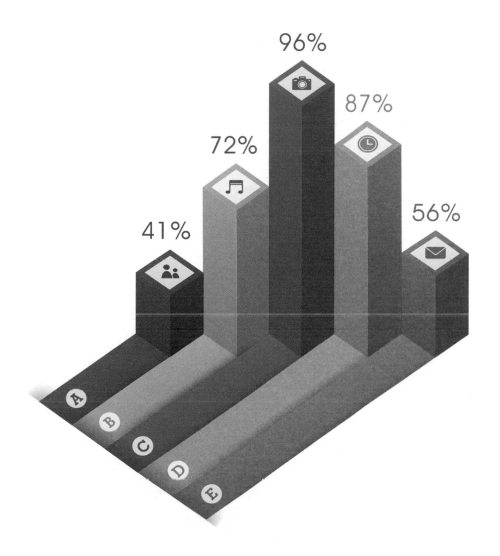

FACTORS OF NUMBERS 1–100

1	1	**26**	1, 2, 13, 26	**51**	1, 3, 17, 51	**76**	1, 2, 4, 19, 38, 76
2	1, 2	**27**	1, 3, 9, 27	**52**	1, 2, 4, 13, 26, 52	**77**	1, 7, 11, 77
3	1, 3	**28**	1, 2, 4, 7, 14, 28	**53**	1, 53	**78**	1, 2, 3, 6, 13, 26, 39, 78
4	1, 2, 4	**29**	1, 29	**54**	1, 2, 3, 6, 9, 18, 27, 54	**79**	1, 79
5	1, 5	**30**	1, 2, 3, 5, 6, 10, 15, 30	**55**	1, 5, 11, 55	**80**	1, 2, 4, 5, 8, 10, 16, 20, 40, 80
6	1, 2, 3, 6	**31**	1, 31	**56**	1, 2, 4, 7, 8, 14, 28, 56	**81**	1, 3, 9, 27, 81
7	1, 7	**32**	1, 2, 4, 8, 16, 32	**57**	1, 3, 19, 57	**82**	1, 2, 41, 82
8	1, 2, 4, 8	**33**	1, 3, 11, 33	**58**	1, 2, 29, 58	**83**	1, 83
9	1, 3, 9	**34**	1, 2, 17, 34	**59**	1, 59	**84**	1, 2, 3, 4, 6, 7, 12, 14, 21, 28, 42, 84
10	1, 2, 5, 10	**35**	1, 5, 7, 35	**60**	1, 2, 3, 4, 5, 6, 10, 12, 15, 20, 30, 60	**85**	1, 5, 17, 85
11	1, 11	**36**	1, 2, 3, 4, 6, 9, 12, 18, 36	**61**	1, 61	**86**	1, 2, 43, 86
12	1, 2, 3, 4, 6, 12	**37**	1, 37	**62**	1, 2, 31, 62	**87**	1, 3, 29, 87
13	1, 13	**38**	1, 2, 19, 38	**63**	1, 3, 7, 9, 21, 63	**88**	1, 2, 4, 8, 11, 22, 44, 88
14	1, 2, 7, 14	**39**	1, 3, 13, 39	**64**	1, 2, 4, 8, 16, 32, 64	**89**	1, 89
15	1, 3, 5, 15	**40**	1, 2, 4, 5, 8, 10, 20, 40	**65**	1, 5, 13, 65	**90**	1, 2, 3, 5, 6, 9, 10, 15, 18, 30, 45, 90
16	1, 2, 4, 8, 16	**41**	1, 41	**66**	1, 2, 3, 6, 11, 22, 33, 66	**91**	1, 7, 13, 91
17	1, 17	**42**	1, 2, 3, 6, 7, 14, 21, 42	**67**	1, 67	**92**	1, 2, 4, 23, 46, 92
18	1, 2, 3, 6, 9, 18	**43**	1, 43	**68**	1, 2, 4, 17, 34, 68	**93**	1, 3, 31, 93
19	1, 19	**44**	1, 2, 4, 11, 22, 44	**69**	1, 3, 23, 69	**94**	1, 2, 47, 94
20	1, 2, 4, 5, 10, 20	**45**	1, 3, 5, 9, 15, 45	**70**	1, 2, 5, 7, 10, 14, 35, 70	**95**	1, 5, 19, 95
21	1, 3, 7, 21	**46**	1, 2, 23, 46	**71**	1, 71	**96**	1, 2, 3, 4, 6, 8, 12, 16, 24, 32, 48, 96
22	1, 2, 11, 22	**47**	1, 47	**72**	1, 2, 3, 4, 6, 8, 9, 12, 18, 24, 36, 72	**97**	1, 97
23	1, 23	**48**	1, 2, 3, 4, 6, 8, 12, 16, 24, 48	**73**	1, 73	**98**	1, 2, 7, 14, 49, 98
24	1, 2, 3, 4, 6, 8, 12, 24	**49**	1, 7, 49	**74**	1, 2, 37, 74	**99**	1, 3, 9, 11, 33, 99
25	1, 5, 25	**50**	1, 2, 5, 10, 25, 50	**75**	1, 3, 5, 15, 25, 75	**100**	1, 2, 4, 5, 10, 20, 25, 50, 100

FRACTION, DECIMAL, AND PERCENT EQUIVALENTS

Fraction	Decimal	Percent	Fraction	Decimal	Percent
1/25	.04	4%	2/5	.4	40%
1/20	.05	5%	7/16	.4375	43.75%
1/16	.0625	6.25%	1/2	.5	50%
1/15	.0̄6	6⅔%	9/16	.5625	56.25%
1/12	.08̄3	8⅓%	3/5	.6	60%
1/10	.1	10%	5/8	.625	62.5%
1/8	.125	12.5%	2/3	.66	66⅔%
1/7	.14̄2857	14%	11/16	.6875	68.75%
1/6	.1̄66	16⅔%	7/10	.7	70%
3/16	.1875	18.75%	3/4	.75	75%
1/5	.2	20%	4/5	.8	80%
1/4	.25	25%	13/16	.8125	81.25%
3/10	.3	30%	7/8	.875	87.5%
5/16	.3125	31.25%	9/10	.9	90%
1/3	.3̄33	33⅓%	15/16	.9375	93.75%
3/8	.375	37.5%	1	1.0	100%

MULTIPLES OF NUMBERS 1–50

1	1, 2, 3, 4, 5, 6, 7, 8, 9 . . .	**26**	26, 52, 78, 104, 130, 156, 182, 208, 234 . . .
2	2, 4, 6, 8, 10, 12, 14, 16, 18 . . .	**27**	27, 54, 81, 108, 135, 162, 189, 216, 243 . . .
3	3, 6, 9, 12, 15, 18, 21, 24, 27 . . .	**28**	28, 56, 84, 112, 140, 168, 196, 224, 252 . . .
4	4, 8, 12, 16, 20, 24, 28, 32, 36 . . .	**29**	29, 58, 87, 116, 145, 174, 203, 232, 261 . . .
5	5, 10, 15, 20, 25, 30, 35, 40, 45 . . .	**30**	30, 60, 90, 120, 150, 180, 210, 240, 270 . . .
6	6, 12, 18, 24, 30, 36, 42, 48, 54 . . .	**31**	31, 62, 93, 124, 155, 186, 217, 248, 279 . . .
7	7, 14, 21, 28, 35, 42, 49, 56, 63 . . .	**32**	32, 64, 96, 128, 160, 192, 224, 256, 288 . . .
8	8, 16, 24, 32, 40, 48, 56, 64, 72 . . .	**33**	33, 66, 99, 132, 165, 198, 231, 264, 297 . . .
9	9, 18, 27, 36, 45, 54, 63, 72, 81 . . .	**34**	34, 68, 102, 136, 170, 204, 238, 272, 306 . . .
10	10, 20, 30, 40, 50, 60, 70, 80, 90 . . .	**35**	35, 70, 105, 140, 175, 210, 245, 280, 315 . . .
11	11, 22, 33, 44, 55, 66, 77, 88, 99 . . .	**36**	36, 72, 108, 144, 180, 216, 252, 288, 324 . . .
12	12, 24, 36, 48, 60, 72, 84, 96, 108 . . .	**37**	37, 74, 111, 148, 185, 222, 259, 296, 333 . . .
13	13, 26, 39, 52, 65, 78, 91, 104, 117 . . .	**38**	38, 76, 114, 152, 190, 228, 266, 304, 342 . . .
14	14, 28, 42, 56, 70, 84, 98, 112, 126 . . .	**39**	39, 78, 117, 156, 195, 234, 273, 312, 351 . . .
15	15, 30, 45, 60, 75, 90, 105, 120, 135 . . .	**40**	40, 80, 120, 160, 200, 240, 280, 320, 360 . . .
16	16, 32, 48, 64, 80, 96, 112, 128, 144 . . .	**41**	41, 82, 123, 164, 205, 246, 287, 328, 369 . . .
17	17, 34, 51, 68, 85, 102, 119, 136, 153 . . .	**42**	42, 84, 126, 168, 210, 252, 294, 336, 378 . . .
18	18, 36, 54, 72, 90, 108, 126, 144, 162 . . .	**43**	43, 86, 129, 172, 215, 258, 301, 344, 387 . . .
19	19, 38, 57, 76, 95, 114, 133, 152, 171 . . .	**44**	44, 88, 132, 176, 220, 264, 308, 352, 396 . . .
20	20, 40, 60, 80, 100, 120, 140, 160, 180 . . .	**45**	45, 90, 135, 180, 225, 270, 315, 360, 405 . . .
21	21, 42, 63, 84, 105, 126, 147, 168, 189 . . .	**46**	46, 92, 138, 184, 230, 276, 322, 368, 414 . . .
22	22, 44, 66, 88, 110, 132, 154, 176, 198 . . .	**47**	47, 94, 141, 188, 235, 282, 329, 376, 423 . . .
23	23, 46, 69, 92, 115, 138, 161, 184, 207 . . .	**48**	48, 96, 144, 192, 240, 288, 336, 384, 432 . . .
24	24, 48, 72, 96, 120, 144, 168, 192, 216 . . .	**49**	49, 98, 147, 196, 245, 294, 343, 392, 441 . . .
25	25, 50, 75, 100, 125, 150, 175, 200, 225 . . .	**50**	50, 100, 150, 200, 250, 300, 350, 400, 450 . . .

MULTIPLES OF NUMBERS 51–100

51	51, 102, 153, 204, 255, 306, 357, 408, 459 . . .	**76**	76, 152, 228, 304, 380, 456, 532, 608, 684 . . .
52	52, 104, 156, 208, 260, 312, 364, 416, 468 . . .	**77**	77, 154, 231, 308, 385, 462, 539, 616, 693 . . .
53	53, 106, 159, 212, 265, 318, 371, 424, 477 . . .	**78**	78, 156, 234, 312, 390, 468, 546, 624, 702 . . .
54	54, 108, 162, 216, 270, 324, 378, 432, 486 . . .	**79**	79, 158, 237, 316, 395, 474, 553, 632, 711 . . .
55	55, 110, 165, 220, 275, 330, 385, 440, 495 . . .	**80**	80, 160, 240, 320, 400, 480, 560, 640, 720 . . .
56	56, 112, 168, 224, 280, 336, 392, 448, 504 . . .	**81**	81, 162, 243, 324, 405, 486, 567, 648, 729 . . .
57	57, 114, 171, 228, 285, 342, 399, 456, 513 . . .	**82**	82, 164, 246, 328, 410, 492, 574, 656, 738 . . .
58	58, 116, 174, 232, 290, 348, 406, 464, 522 . . .	**83**	83, 166, 249, 332, 415, 498, 581, 664, 747 . . .
59	59, 118, 177, 236, 295, 354, 413, 472, 531 . . .	**84**	84, 168, 252, 336, 420, 504, 588, 672, 756 . . .
60	60, 120, 180, 240, 300, 360, 420, 480, 540 . . .	**85**	85, 170, 255, 340, 425, 510, 595, 680, 765 . . .
61	61, 122, 183, 244, 305, 366, 427, 488, 549 . . .	**86**	86, 172, 258, 344, 430, 516, 602, 688, 774 . . .
62	62, 124, 186, 248, 310, 372, 434, 496, 558 . . .	**87**	87, 174, 261, 348, 435, 522, 609, 696, 783 . . .
63	63, 126, 189, 252, 315, 378, 441, 504, 567 . . .	**88**	88, 176, 264, 352, 440, 528, 616, 704, 792 . . .
64	64, 128, 192, 256, 320, 384, 448, 512, 576 . . .	**89**	89, 178, 267, 356, 445, 534, 623, 712, 801 . . .
65	65, 130, 195, 260, 325, 390, 455, 520, 585 . . .	**90**	90, 180, 270, 360, 450, 540, 630, 720, 810 . . .
66	66, 132, 198, 264, 330, 396, 462, 528, 594 . . .	**91**	91, 182, 273, 364, 455, 546, 637, 728, 819 . . .
67	67, 134, 201, 268, 335, 402, 469, 536, 603 . . .	**92**	92, 184, 276, 368, 460, 552, 644, 736, 828 . . .
68	68, 136, 204, 272, 340, 408, 476, 544, 612 . . .	**93**	93, 186, 279, 372, 465, 558, 651, 744, 837 . . .
69	69, 138, 207, 276, 345, 414, 483, 552, 621 . . .	**94**	94, 188, 282, 376, 470, 564, 658, 752, 846 . . .
70	70, 140, 210, 280, 350, 420, 490, 560, 630 . . .	**95**	95, 190, 285, 380, 475, 570, 665, 760, 855 . . .
71	71, 142, 213, 284, 355, 426, 497, 568, 639 . . .	**96**	96, 192, 288, 384, 480, 576, 672, 768, 864 . . .
72	72, 144, 216, 288, 360, 432, 504, 576, 648 . . .	**97**	97, 194, 291, 388, 485, 582, 679, 776, 873 . . .
73	73, 146, 219, 292, 365, 438, 511, 584, 657 . . .	**98**	98, 196, 294, 392, 490, 588, 686, 784, 882 . . .
74	74, 148, 222, 296, 370, 444, 518, 592, 666 . . .	**99**	99, 198, 297, 396, 495, 594, 693, 792, 891 . . .
75	75, 150, 225, 300, 375, 450, 525, 600, 675 . . .	**100**	100, 200, 300, 400, 500, 600, 700, 800, 900 . . .

MULTIPLICATION CHART

x	1	2	3	4	5	6	7	8	9	10	11	12
1	1	2	3	4	5	6	7	8	9	10	11	12
2	2	4	6	8	10	12	14	16	18	20	22	24
3	3	6	9	12	15	18	21	24	27	30	33	36
4	4	8	12	16	20	24	28	32	36	40	44	48
5	5	10	15	20	25	30	35	40	45	50	55	60
6	6	12	18	24	30	36	42	48	54	60	66	72
7	7	14	21	28	35	42	49	56	63	70	77	84
8	8	16	24	32	40	48	56	64	72	80	88	96
9	9	18	27	36	45	54	63	72	81	90	99	108
10	10	20	30	40	50	60	70	80	90	100	110	120
11	11	22	33	44	55	66	77	88	99	110	121	132
12	12	24	36	48	60	72	84	96	108	120	132	144

PRIME FACTORS OF NUMBERS 2–100

2	prime	27	3 • 3 • 3	52	2 • 2 • 13	77	7 • 11
3	prime	28	2 • 2 • 7	53	prime	78	2 • 3 • 13
4	2 • 2	29	prime	54	2 • 3 • 3 • 3	79	prime
5	prime	30	2 • 3 • 5	55	5 • 11	80	2 • 2 • 2 • 2 • 5
6	2 • 3	31	prime	56	2 • 2 • 2 • 7	81	3 • 3 • 3 • 3
7	prime	32	2 • 2 • 2 • 2 • 2	57	3 • 19	82	2 • 41
8	2 • 2 • 2	33	3 • 11	58	2 • 29	83	prime
9	3 • 3	34	2 • 17	59	prime	84	2 • 2 • 3 • 7
10	2 • 5	35	5 • 7	60	2 • 2 • 3 • 5	85	5 • 17
11	prime	36	2 • 2 • 3 • 3	61	prime	86	2 • 43
12	2 • 2 • 3	37	prime	62	2 • 31	87	3 • 29
13	prime	38	2 • 19	63	3 • 3 • 7	88	2 • 2 • 2 • 11
14	2 • 7	39	3 • 13	64	2 • 2 • 2 • 2 • 2 • 2	89	prime
15	3 • 5	40	2 • 2 • 2 • 5	65	5 • 13	90	2 • 3 • 3 • 5
16	2 • 2 • 2 • 2	41	prime	66	2 • 3 • 11	91	7 • 13
17	prime	42	2 • 3 • 7	67	prime	92	2 • 2 • 23
18	2 • 3 • 3	43	prime	68	2 • 2 • 17	93	3 • 31
19	prime	44	2 • 2 • 11	69	3 • 23	94	2 • 47
20	2 • 2 • 5	45	3 • 3 • 5	70	2 • 5 • 7	95	5 • 19
21	3 • 7	46	2 • 23	71	prime	96	2 • 2 • 2 • 2 • 2 • 3
22	2 • 11	47	prime	72	2 • 2 • 2 • 3 • 3	97	prime
23	prime	48	2 • 2 • 2 • 2 • 3	73	prime	98	2 • 7 • 7
24	2 • 2 • 2 • 3	49	7 • 7	74	2 • 37	99	3 • 3 • 11
25	5 • 5	50	2 • 5 • 5	75	3 • 5 • 5	100	2 • 2 • 5 • 5
26	2 • 13	51	3 • 17	76	2 • 2 • 19		

PRIME NUMBER CHART

To find prime numbers:
1. Cross off 1.
2. Circle 2, 3, 5, and 7.
3. Cross off all of the remaining multiples of 2, 3, 5, and 7.
4. Circle the numbers that are left. These are the prime numbers.

1	2	3	4	5	6	7	8	9	10
11	12	13	14	15	16	17	18	19	20
21	22	23	24	25	26	27	28	29	30
31	32	33	34	35	36	37	38	39	40
41	42	43	44	45	46	47	48	49	50
51	52	53	54	55	56	57	58	59	60
61	62	63	64	65	66	67	68	69	70
71	72	73	74	75	76	77	78	79	80
81	82	83	84	85	86	87	88	89	90
91	92	93	94	95	96	97	98	99	100

SQUARES AND SQUARE ROOTS

n	n^2		n	n^2	
1	1	1	26	676	5.099
2	4	1.414	27	729	5.196
3	9	1.732	28	784	5.292
4	16	2	29	841	5.385
5	25	2.236	30	900	5.477
6	36	2.45	31	961	5.568
7	49	2.646	32	1024	5.657
8	64	2.828	33	1089	5.745
9	81	3	34	1156	5.831
10	100	3.162	35	1225	5.916
11	121	3.317	36	1296	6
12	144	3.464	37	1369	6.083
13	169	3.606	38	1444	6.164
14	196	3.742	39	1521	6.245
15	225	3.873	40	1600	6.325
16	256	4	41	1681	6.403
17	289	4.123	42	1764	6.481
18	324	4.243	43	1849	6.557
19	361	4.359	44	1936	6.633
20	400	4.472	45	2025	6.708
21	441	4.583	46	2116	6.782
22	484	4.69	47	2209	6.856
23	529	4.796	48	2304	6.928
24	576	4.899	49	2401	7
25	625	5	50	2500	7,071

MEASUREMENT CONVERSION TABLES

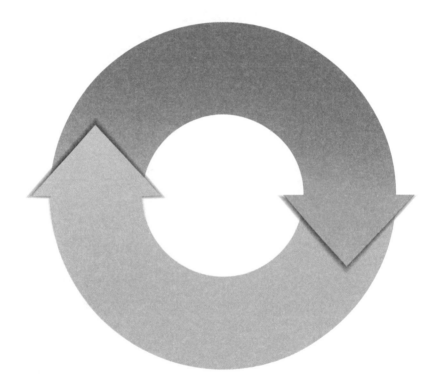

BASIC FORMULAS

to change				to change			
inches	▸	millimeters	▸▸ x 25.4	pounds	▸	grams	▸▸ x 453.59
millimeters	▸	inches	▸▸ x 0.0394	grams	▸	pounds	▸▸ x 0.002205
inches	▸	centimeters	▸▸ x 2.54	pounds	▸	kilograms	▸▸ x 0.45359
centimeters	▸	inches	▸▸ x 0.3937	kilograms	▸	pounds	▸▸ 2.205
feet	▸	meters	▸▸ x 0.3048	ounces	▸	liters	▸▸ x 0.0296
meters	▸	feet	▸▸ x 3.281	ounce	▸	cubic inches	▸▸ x 1.878
yards	▸	meters	▸▸ x 0.9144	pint	▸	liters	▸▸ x 0.4731
meters	▸	yards	▸▸ x 1.094	liters	▸	pints	▸▸ x 2.114
miles	▸	kilometers	▸▸ x 1.609	cubic inches	▸	pints	▸▸ x 0.0347
kilometers	▸	miles	▸▸ x 0.6214	pints	▸	cubic inches	▸▸ x 28.88
knots	▸	kilometers	▸▸ x 1.852	quarts	▸	liters	▸▸ x 0.9463
knots	▸	miles	▸▸ x 1.150779	gallons	▸	liters	▸▸ x 3.785
ounces	▸	grams	▸▸ x 28.349	liters	▸	gallons	▸▸ x 0.2642
grams	▸	ounces	▸▸ x 0.03527				

CELSIUS

freezing point of water = 0° C					
boiling point of water = 100° C					
To convert Celsius to Fahrenheit: C x ⅘ + 32 = F					

°C	°F	°C	°F	°C	°F	°C	°F	°C	°F	°C	°F
50	122	36	97	22	72	8	46	−6	21	−20	−4
49	120	35	95	21	70	7	45	−7	19	−21	−6
48	118	34	93	20	68	6	43	−8	18	−22	−8
47	117	33	91	19	66	5	41	−9	16	−23	−9
46	115	32	90	18	64	4	39	−10	14	−24	−11
45	113	31	88	17	63	3	37	−11	12	−25	−13
44	111	30	86	16	61	2	36	−12	10	−26	−15
43	109	29	84	15	59	1	34	−13	9	−27	−17
42	108	28	82	14	57	0	32	−14	7	−28	−18
41	106	27	81	13	55	−1	30	−15	5	−29	−20
40	104	26	79	12	54	−2	28	−16	3	−30	−22
39	102	25	77	11	52	−3	27	−17	1	−31	−24
38	100	24	75	10	50	−4	25	−18	−0.4	−32	−26
37	99	23	73	9	48	−5	23	−19	−2	−33	−27

FAHRENHEIT

freezing point of water = 32° F	
boiling point of water = 212° C	

To convert Fahrenheit to Celsius: (F – 32) x ⅝ = C

°F	°C	°F	°C	°F	°C	°F	°C	°F	°C	°F	°C
110	43	90	32	70	21	50	10	30	−1	10	−12
109	43	89	32	69	21	49	9	29	−2	9	−13
108	42	88	31	68	20	48	9	28	−2	8	−13
107	42	87	31	67	19	47	8	27	−3	7	−14
106	41	86	30	66	19	46	8	26	−3	6	−14
105	41	85	29	65	18	45	7	25	−4	5	−15
104	40	84	29	64	18	44	7	24	−4	4	−16
103	39	83	28	63	17	43	6	23	−5	3	−16
102	39	82	28	62	17	42	6	22	−6	2	−17
101	38	81	27	61	16	41	5	21	−6	1	−17
100	38	80	27	60	16	40	4	20	−7	0	−18
99	37	79	26	59	15	39	4	19	−7	−1	−18
98	37	78	26	58	14	38	3	18	−8	−2	−19
97	36	77	25	57	14	37	3	17	−8	−3	−19
96	36	76	24	56	13	36	2	16	−9	−4	−20
95	35	75	24	55	13	35	2	15	−9	−5	−21
94	34	74	23	54	12	34	1	14	−10	−6	−21
93	34	73	23	53	12	33	0.6	13	−11	−7	−22
92	33	72	22	52	11	32	0	12	−11	−8	−22
91	33	71	22	51	11	31	−0.6	11	−12	−9	−23

KILOGRAMS

There are 1,000 grams in a kilogram. 1 kilogram = 2.2046 pounds											
Multiply kilograms by 2.2046 = pounds						1 kilogram = the weight of about 1 liter of water					
kg	**lbs**	**kg**	**lbs**	**kg**	**lbs**	**kg**	**lbs**	**kg**	**lbs**	**kg**	**lbs**
1	2.20	**21**	46.30	**41**	90.39	**61**	134.48	**81**	178.57	**101**	222.67
2	4.41	**22**	48.50	**42**	92.59	**62**	136.69	**82**	180.78	**102**	224.87
3	6.61	**23**	50.71	**43**	94.80	**63**	138.89	**83**	182.98	**103**	227.08
4	8.82	**24**	52.91	**44**	97.00	**64**	141.10	**84**	185.19	**104**	229.28
5	11.02	**25**	55.12	**45**	99.21	**65**	143.30	**85**	187.39	**105**	231.49
6	13.23	**26**	57.32	**46**	101.41	**66**	145.50	**86**	189.60	**106**	233.69
7	15.43	**27**	59.52	**47**	103.62	**67**	147.71	**87**	191.80	**107**	235.89
8	17.64	**28**	61.73	**48**	105.82	**68**	149.91	**88**	194.01	**108**	238.10
9	19.84	**29**	63.93	**49**	108.03	**69**	152.12	**89**	196.21	**109**	240.30
10	22.05	**30**	66.14	**50**	110.23	**70**	154.32	**90**	198.42	**110**	242.51
11	24.25	**31**	68.34	**51**	112.44	**71**	156.53	**91**	200.62	**111**	244.71
12	26.46	**32**	70.55	**52**	114.64	**72**	158.73	**92**	202.83	**112**	246.92
13	28.66	**33**	72.75	**53**	116.84	**73**	160.94	**93**	205.03	**113**	249.12
14	30.86	**34**	74.96	**54**	119.05	**74**	163.14	**94**	207.23	**114**	251.33
15	33.07	**35**	77.16	**55**	121.25	**75**	165.35	**95**	209.44	**115**	253.53
16	35.27	**36**	79.37	**56**	123.46	**76**	167.55	**96**	211.64	**116**	255.74
17	37.48	**37**	81.57	**57**	125.66	**77**	169.76	**97**	213.85	**117**	257.94
18	39.68	**38**	83.78	**58**	127.87	**78**	171.96	**98**	216.05	**118**	260.15
19	41.89	**39**	85.98	**59**	130.07	**79**	174.16	**99**	218.26	**119**	262.35
20	44.09	**40**	88.18	**60**	132.28	**80**	176.37	**100**	220.46	**120**	264.55

KILOMETERS

There are 1,000 meters in a kilometer.
1 kilometer = 0.6214 mile = 3,280 feet

1 kilometer = 0.6214 miles Multiply kilometers by 0.6214 = mph						1 kilometer = 0.53996 knots Multiply kilometers by 0.53996 = knots					
km/hr	mph	knots	km/hr	mph	knots	km/hr	mph	knots	km/hr	mph	knots
1	.62	0.5	14	8.7	7.6	27	16.8	14.6	40	24.9	21.6
2	1.2	1.1	15	9.3	8.1	28	17.4	15.1	41	25.5	22.1
3	1.9	1.6	16	9.9	8.6	29	18.0	15.7	42	26.1	22.7
4	2.5	2.2	17	10.6	9.2	30	18.6	16.2	43	26.7	23.2
5	3.1	2.7	18	11.2	9.7	31	19.3	16.7	44	27.3	23.8
6	3.7	3.2	19	11.8	10.3	32	19.9	17.3	45	28.0	24.3
7	4.4	3.8	20	12.4	10.8	33	20.5	17.8	46	28.6	24.8
8	5.0	4.3	21	13.0	11.3	34	21.1	18.4	47	29.2	25.4
9	5.6	4.9	22	13.7	11.9	35	21.7	18.9	48	29.8	25.9
10	6.2	5.4	23	14.3	12.4	36	22.4	19.4	49	30.4	26.5
11	6.8	5.9	24	14.9	13.0	37	23.0	20.0	50	31.1	27.0
12	7.5	6.5	25	15.5	13.5	38	23.6	20.5	51	31.7	27.5
13	8.1	7.0	26	16.2	14.0	39	24.2	21.1	52	32.3	28.1

KNOTS

Knots are nautical miles per hour. 1 nautical mile = 6076.12 feet = 1852 meters											
1 nautical mile/knot = 1.15077945 statute mile Multiply knots by 1.15077945 = mph						1 knot/nautical mile = 1.85200 kilometers Multiply knots by 1.85200 = kilometers					
Knots	mph	km/hr	Knots	mph	km/hr	Knots	mph	km/hr	Knots	mph	km/hr
1	1.2	1.9	14	16.1	25.9	27	31.1	50.0	40	46.0	74.1
2	2.3	3.7	15	17.3	27.8	28	32.2	51.9	41	47.2	75.9
3	3.5	5.6	16	18.4	29.6	29	33.4	53.7	42	48.3	77.8
4	4.6	7.4	17	19.6	31.5	30	34.5	55.6	43	49.5	79.6
5	5.8	9.3	18	20.7	33.3	31	35.7	57.4	44	50.6	81.5
6	6.9	11.1	19	21.9	35.2	32	36.8	59.3	45	51.8	83.3
7	8.1	13.0	20	23.0	37.0	33	38.0	61.1	46	52.9	85.2
8	9.2	14.8	21	24.2	38.9	34	39.1	63.0	47	54.1	87.0
9	10.4	16.7	22	25.3	40.7	35	40.3	64.8	48	55.2	88.9
10	11.5	18.5	23	26.5	42.6	36	41.4	66.7	49	56.4	90.7
11	12.7	20.4	24	27.6	44.4	37	42.6	68.5	50	57.5	92.6
12	13.8	22.2	25	28.8	46.3	38	43.7	70.4	51	58.7	94.5
13	15.0	24.1	26	29.9	48.2	39	44.9	72.2	52	59.8	96.3

MILES

There are 5280 feet in a mile. 1 mile = 1.6093 kilometers = 1,609.3 meters											
1 mile = 1.6093 kilometers Multiply miles by 1.6093 = kilometers						1 mile = 0.86898 knots/nautical miles Multiply miles by 0.86898 = knots					
Miles	km/ hr	knots	**Miles**	km/ hr	knots	**Miles**	km/ hr	knots	**Miles**	km/ hr	knots
1	1.6	0.9	**14**	22.5	12.2	**27**	43.5	23.5	**40**	64.4	34.8
2	3.2	1.7	**15**	24.1	13.0	**28**	45.1	24.3	**41**	66.0	35.6
3	4.8	2.6	**16**	25.7	13.9	**29**	46.7	25.2	**42**	67.6	36.5
4	6.4	3.5	**17**	27.4	14.8	**30**	48.3	26.1	**43**	69.2	37.4
5	8.0	4.3	**18**	29.0	15.6	**31**	49.9	26.9	**44**	70.8	38.2
6	9.7	5.2	**19**	30.6	16.5	**32**	51.5	27.8	**45**	72.4	39.1
7	11.3	6.1	**20**	32.2	17.4	**33**	53.1	28.7	**46**	74.0	40.0
8	12.9	7.0	**21**	33.8	18.2	**34**	54.7	29.5	**47**	75.6	40.8
9	14.5	7.8	**22**	35.4	19.1	**35**	56.3	30.4	**48**	77.2	41.7
10	16.1	8.7	**23**	37.0	20.0	**36**	57.9	31.3	**49**	78.9	42.6
11	17.7	9.6	**24**	38.6	20.9	**37**	59.5	32.2	**50**	80.5	43.4
12	19.3	10.4	**25**	40.2	21.7	**38**	61.2	33.0	**51**	82.1	44.3
13	20.9	11.3	**26**	41.8	22.6	**39**	62.8	33.9	**52**	83.7	45.2

POUNDS

There are 16 ounces in a pound. 1 pound = 0.4536 kilograms											
Multiply pounds by 0.4536 = kilograms						2,000 pounds = 1 ton					
lbs	kg	lbs	kg	lbs	kg	lbs	kg	lbs	kg	lbs	kg
1	0.45	21	9.53	41	18.60	61	27.67	81	36.74	101	45.81
2	0.91	22	9.98	42	19.05	62	28.12	82	37.20	102	46.27
3	1.36	23	10.43	43	19.50	63	28.58	83	37.65	103	46.72
4	1.81	24	10.89	44	19.96	64	29.03	84	38.10	104	47.17
5	2.27	25	11.34	45	20.41	65	29.48	85	38.56	105	47.63
6	2.72	26	11.79	46	20.87	66	29.94	86	39.01	106	48.08
7	3.18	27	12.25	47	21.32	67	30.39	87	39.46	107	48.54
8	3.63	28	12.70	48	21.77	68	30.84	88	39.92	108	48.99
9	4.08	29	13.15	49	22.23	69	31.30	89	40.37	109	49.44
10	4.54	30	13.61	50	22.68	70	31.75	90	40.82	110	49.90
11	4.99	31	14.06	51	23.13	71	32.21	91	41.28	111	50.35
12	5.44	32	14.52	52	23.59	72	32.66	92	41.73	112	50.80
13	5.90	33	14.97	53	24.04	73	33.11	93	42.18	113	51.26
14	6.35	34	15.42	54	24.49	74	33.57	94	42.64	114	51.71
15	6.80	35	15.88	55	24.95	75	34.02	95	43.09	115	52.16
16	7.26	36	16.33	56	25.40	76	34.47	96	43.55	116	52.62
17	7.71	37	16.78	57	25.86	77	34.93	97	44.00	117	53.07
18	8.16	38	17.24	58	26.31	78	35.38	98	44.45	118	53.52
19	8.62	39	17.69	59	26.76	79	35.83	99	44.91	119	53.98
20	9.07	40	18.14	60	27.22	80	36.29	100	45.36	120	54.43

TRIVIA

1 fathom = 6 feet = 1.829 meters	A knot is the measure of speed on water	1 knot is 1 nautical mile per hour	1 nautical mile = 6,080 feet = 1852 meters	1 nautical mile = 1.15 miles = 1.852 kilometers
1 gallon of gasoline weighs 6.2 pounds	1 gallon of diesel weighs 7.1 pounds	1 cubic foot of volume holds 7.48 gallons	1 cubic foot of volume will support about 60 pounds	1 cubic foot of fresh water weighs 62.5 pounds
1 statute mile = 1.609 kilometers = 1,609 meters	1 statute mile = 1,760 yards = 5,280 feet	1 kilometer = 1,000 meters	1 kilometer = 0.6142 miles = 3,290 feet	1 meter = 3.281 feet = 39.37 inches
1 yard = 0.9144 meters	1 pound = 0.45359 kilograms	1 gallon (liquid) = 3.7854 liters	1 foot = 0.3048 meters	1 inch = 2.54 centimeters

BASIC MATH TOOLS AND EQUIPMENT

BASIC MATH TOOLS AND EQUIPMENT

Although the possibilities for manipulatives are almost as limitless as the imagination, below are a few of those most commonly found in math classrooms.

AngLegs™

Anglegs™ are a set of plastic pieces in six different lengths that snap together to make various geometric shapes. These are useful for exploring polygons and angles. They can also be used to determine polygon height, area, center points, and more.

Attribute Blocks

A set of geometric shapes of various sizes and thicknesses. These can be used to learn shape recognition, patterning, spatial sense, sorting, classifying, and logical reasoning in problem solving.

Balance Scale

A tool used for measuring. Balance scales have two buckets or pans, one on each side of a balance beam. The center of the beam usually has a needle to show equality. When each pan contains exactly the same mass, the beam will balance. Objects can be balanced against each other, or a set of weights can be used to find the weight of something.

BASIC MATH TOOLS AND EQUIPMENT

Base-10 Blocks

Manipulatives based on the Base-10 number system. Three of the most commonly used pieces are very effective tools for learning counting, place value, number sense, addition, subtraction, multiplication, division, and decimals.

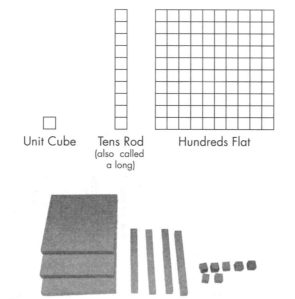

Unit Cube   Tens Rod
(also called
a long)
   Hundreds Flat

Centimeter Cubes

Cubes that measure one centimeter in length, width, and height. They are useful for metric measurement and weight, as well as finding volume and surface area and in problem solving.

Compass

A tool used for drawing arcs and circles. One type has two hinged arms. One arm is pointed at the end, while the other holds a pencil. The other type of compass is called a safety compass and consists of a wider arm that rotates around a circular base.

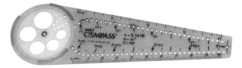

Cuisenaire® Rods

Cuisenaire® Rods are a set of 10 different-colored rods used to learn a wide variety of concepts, including addition, subtraction, multiplication, division, fractions, area, perimeter, volume, spatial problem solving, square numbers, and equations. Based on a unit cube, these range in size from 1 unit (white) to 10 units (orange).

BASIC MATH TOOLS AND EQUIPMENT

Dice

Dice come in a variety of colors and shapes and are numbered in a variety of ways, including the standard form, fractions, and decimals. They can be used in countless ways, such as for addition and subtraction facts, multiplication facts, fraction concepts and equivalences, probability, graphing, and a wide assortment of math games.

Dominoes

Dominoes come in the traditional black and white, as well as a variety of colors. They are used to build number sense, compose and decompose numbers, addition and subtraction concepts, fact families, and multiples.

Dot Paper

Paper filled with evenly spaced dots used to solve and record answers to geometry problems, especially those involving shapes, angles, and parts of circles. Dot paper is also commonly called geoboard paper.

Fraction Sets

Fraction sets come in a variety of shapes and sizes. As their name implies, fraction sets are useful tools for learning fraction concepts.

Geoboard

Geoboards are square boards with a series of pegs used to explore concepts of plane geometry, including but not limited to area, perimeter, line segments, angles, properties of plane shapes, and the characteristics of circles. Rubber bands, sometimes called geobands, are used to model the desired concepts. Some geoboards are fitted with a series of pegs in the shape of a grid on one side, while the other side has pegs in the shape of a circle. Geoboards are commonly used with dot paper.

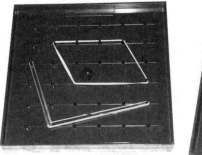
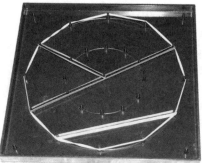

Geoboard Paper

See *Dot Paper*.

Geometric Solids

A set of three-dimensional pieces used to explore the properties of dimensional geometric shapes. Although there are many other dimensional shapes, many sets commonly include cubes, rectangular prisms, triangular prisms, cylinders, cones, square pyramids, triangular pyramids, rectangular pyramids, tetrahedrons, and spheres. Some sets are hollow to allow for an exploration of volume, surface area, and nets.

Graph Paper

Paper separated into grids of various sizes. Graph paper can be used in basic operations to help keep problems lined up and in the exploration of multiplication and division, area, perimeter, and shapes.

Hundreds Charts

A chart set up in a grid and numbered to teach various concepts. Some are numbered from 1 to 100, others start with zero, and still others start with a negative number. These are used to explore patterning, counting strategies, addition, subtraction, multiples, common multiples, prime numbers, and negative numbers.

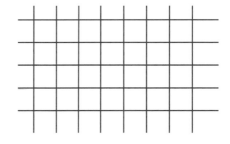

1	2	3	4	5	6	7	8	9	10
11	12	13	14	15	16	17	18	19	20
21	22	23	24	25	26	27	28	29	30
31	32	33	34	35	36	37	38	39	40
41	42	43	44	45	46	47	48	49	50
51	52	53	54	55	56	57	58	59	60
61	62	63	64	65	66	67	68	69	70
71	72	73	74	75	76	77	78	79	80
81	82	83	84	85	86	87	88	89	90
91	92	93	94	95	96	97	98	99	100

Inch Cubes

Inch cubes come in a variety of colors. Measuring an inch on each side, these are useful for counting, patterning, volume, and surface area.

Math Gems

Glass drops with a flat bottom. They are fairly inexpensive, very versatile, and can be purchased at many local craft stores. These work well in a variety of circumstances, including building addition, subtraction, multiplication, and division problems; modeling fractions and decimals; and problem solving.

Meter Stick (Metre Stick)

In metric measurement, a meter stick is used to measure lengths of up to one meter. Meter sticks are straight-edged long rulers marked and divided into 100 centimeters, the length of a meter. They are usually further marked by decimeters (10 centimeter increments). One meter equals 3.28 feet, or 39.37 inches.

Mirrors

Mirrors are used to explore line symmetry and to learn the concept of angle measurement. When used in line symmetry, the mirrors are generally one piece. When used with angle measurement, they are commonly taped together to form a hinged pair.

Pattern Blocks

These are used to investigate a multitude of concepts including patterning, area, perimeter, basic fractions, equivalent fractions, adding and subtracting fractions, line symmetry, rotational symmetry, angles, properties of basic shapes, similarity, congruence, and tessellations. A set of pattern blocks comes in a container of about 250 or more and includes six basic shapes: yellow hexagon, red trapezoid, blue rhombus, green triangle, orange square, and tan rhombus.

Pentominoes

A geometric manipulative used to explore area, perimeter, symmetry, congruence, nets, and problem solving. Pentomino puzzles come in a set of 12 shapes, each made of five 1-inch squares.

Protractor

A tool used for drawing and measuring angles, most protractors are designed in the shape of a hemisphere and numbered from 0 to 180 degrees. Full circle protractors are also available, but they are not as commonly used.

BASIC MATH TOOLS AND EQUIPMENT

Spinners

A tool that can be numbered in a variety of increments in number, color, or pattern to suit learning needs. These are often used in probability.

Spring Scale

A measuring tool used to measure weight or force. A hook at the bottom holds the object to be measured. Oftentimes, these are marked in grams and Newtons.

Tangrams

Tangrams consist of seven puzzle pieces that are put together to make a large assortment of shapes. These puzzles can be used to investigate properties of polygons, similarity, congruence, line and rotational symmetry, angles, fractions, area, perimeter, and problem solving. Each puzzle comes with two large triangles, a medium triangle, two small triangles, a square, and a parallelogram.

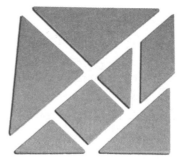

Tape Measure

A flexible type of ruler, often made of cloth, plastic, or fiberglass. It is very useful for measuring curved objects. Some come in standard measurements of inch, foot, and yard; others will be in metric units of millimeters, centimeters, and decimeters. Still others will have standard units on one side and metric units on the other.

Tiles

Tiles are usually 1-inch square manipulatives used in counting, patterning, addition, subtraction, multiplication, division, fractional concepts, and multiplication of fractions.

Two-Color Counters

These are generally about 1 inch in diameter and have a different color on each side. Two-sided counters are used for number sense and operations, patterning, probability, addition, multiplication, division, and fractions.

Unifix Cubes®

Interlocking blocks in a 1-inch size, Unifix Cubes® come in a variety of colors. They can be used for number sense, patterning, addition, subtraction, multiplication, division, and fractions.

Yardstick

In standard measurement, a yardstick is a measuring stick used to measure lengths up to one yard. Yardsticks are straight-edged long rulers marked and divided into 36 inches, the length of a yard. They are usually further marked by feet (12 inches). One yard equals 0.9144 meters.

INDEX

INDEX

INDEX

INDEX

ABOUT THE AUTHOR

Theresa R. Fitzgerald has been a fourth-grade teacher with the Linden Community Schools since 1992, shortly after graduating with a bachelor's degree from the University of Michigan–Flint. She earned her master's degree in math/science elementary education from Eastern Michigan University, and has continued to further her own education through additional courses with Marygrove College and PLS, in addition to participating in various local math workshops. Residing in mid-Michigan, Theresa has worked on curriculum development and teacher training in math and science and has worked as a consultant developing materials and presenting math workshops at the district level and science workshops at the county level. Her latest ventures involve using technology in the classroom.

Theresa's love of math and interest in helping children understand its concepts led to the development of this math dictionary. The need for a math resource to help elementary and middle school children and their parents with terminology and concepts became apparent as Theresa's daughter, Amanda, grew. Initially developed as a Sam's Work project over a period of about 10 years, its use on a daily basis has helped students find sustained success in math.

Theresa and John, her husband of more than 25 years, enjoy as much time as they can on their boat in Lake Huron. They've traveled and explored Canada's North Channel extensively, and look forward to more of the same as the seasons permit.

MATH DICTIONARY FOR KIDS

STANDARDS ALIGNMENT

GRADE LEVEL	COMMON CORE STATE STANDARDS IN MATH
Grade 4	4.OA.A Use the four operations with whole numbers to solve problems.
	4.OA.B Gain familiarity with factors and multiples.
	4.OA.C Generate and analyze patterns.
	4.NBT.A Generalize place value understanding for multi-digit whole numbers.
	4.NBT.B Use place value understanding and properties of operations to perform multi-digit arithmetic.
	4.NF.A Extend understanding of fraction equivalence and ordering.
	4.NF.B Build fractions from unit fractions.
	4.NF.C Understand decimal notation for fractions, and compare decimal fractions.
	4.MD.A Solve problems involving measurement and conversion of measurements.
	4.MD.B Represent and interpret data.
	4.MD.C Geometric measurement: understand concepts of angle and measure angles.
	4.G.A Draw and identify lines and angles, and classify shapes by properties of their lines and angles.
Grade 5	5.OA.A Write and interpret numerical expressions.
	5.OA.B Analyze patterns and relationships.
	5.NBT.A Understand the place value system.
	5.NBT.B Perform operations with multi-digit whole numbers and with decimals to hundredths.
	5.NF.A Use equivalent fractions as a strategy to add and subtract fractions.
	5.NF.B Apply and extend previous understandings of multiplication and division.
	5.MD.A Convert like measurement units within a given measurement system.
	5.MD.B Represent and interpret data.
	5.MD.C Geometric measurement: understand concepts of volume.
	5.G.A Graph points on the coordinate plane to solve real-world and mathematical problems.
	5.G.B Classify two-dimensional figures into categories based on their properties.
Grade 6	6.G.A Solve real-world and mathematical problems involving area, surface area, and volume.
	6.RP.A Understand ratio concepts and use ratio reasoning to solve problems.
	6.NS.A Apply and extend previous understandings of multiplication and division to divide fractions by fractions.
	6.NS.B Compute fluently with multi-digit numbers and find common factors and multiples.
	6.NS.C Apply and extend previous understandings of numbers to the system of rational numbers.

GRADE LEVEL	COMMON CORE STATE STANDARDS IN MATH
Grade 6, *continued*	6.EE.A Apply and extend previous understandings of arithmetic to algebraic expressions.
	6.EE.B Reason about and solve one-variable equations and inequalities.
	6.SP.A Develop understanding of statistical variability.
	6.SP.B Summarize and describe distributions.
Grade 7	7.G.A Draw construct, and describe geometrical figures and describe the relationships between them.
	7.G.B Solve real-life and mathematical problems involving angle measure, area, surface area, and volume.
	7.RP.A Analyze proportional relationships and use them to solve real-world and mathematical problems.
	7.NS.A Apply and extend previous understandings of operations with fractions.
	7.EE.A Use properties of operations to generate equivalent expressions.
	7.EE.B Solve real-life and mathematical problems using numerical and algebraic expressions and equations.
	7.SP.B Draw informal comparative inferences about two populations.
	7.SP.C Investigate chance processes and develop, use, and evaluate probability models.
Grade 8	8.NS.A Know that there are numbers that are not rational, and approximate them by rational numbers.
	8.EE.A Work with radicals and integer exponents.
	8.EE.B Understand the connections between proportional relationships, lines, and linear equations.
	8.F.A Define, evaluate, and compare functions.
	8.F.B Use functions to model relationships between quantities.
	8.SP.A Investigate patterns of association in bivariate data.
	8.G.A Understand congruence and similarity using physical models, transparencies, or geometry software.
	8.G.B Understand and apply the Pythagorean Theorem.
	8.G.C Solve real-world and mathematical problems involving volume of cylinders, cones, and spheres.
Grade 9	HSF-IF.B Interpret functions that arise in applications in terms of the context.
	HSG-CO.A Experiment with transformations in the plane.
	HSG-CO.B Understand congruence in terms of rigid motions.
	HSG-GMD.A Explain volume formulas and use them to solve problems.
	HSG-GMD.B Visualize relationships between two-dimensional and three-dimensional objects.